T0194334

I Never Did Much But I Had Fun Doing It

The Funny Side of Growing Up in a Small Town

BILLY GRAY

WESTBOW
PRESS®
A DIVISION OF THOMAS NELSON
& ZONDERVAN

WestBow Press books may be ordered through booksellers or by contacting:

WestBow Press
A Division of Thomas Nelson & Zondervan
1663 Liberty Drive
Bloomington, IN 47403
www.westbowpress.com
1 (866) 928-1240

ISBN: 978-1-9736-6495-6 (sc)
ISBN: 978-1-9736-6494-9 (e)

Print information available on the last page.

WestBow Press rev. date: 07/02/2019

Contents

Introduction to Fun

When I Was a Boy

THE WORLD I LIVED in as a boy was not like the world kids grow up in today. For instance, when I was a boy...

...Flattop haircuts were the craze. The only guys who didn't get the close shave were the fellows who wore the ducktail cut so they could look like Elvis or the nerds who parted their hair either on the side or in the middle or those guys with such wavy hair that it would have killed their moms to have it cut off. But the rest of us guys were into flattops big time and the resident flattop expert in our town was a Mr. Hickman who worked at Lamb's Barber Shop.

...Coke bottles were only 6.5 ounces and made of glass. The best ones were out of the drink machine because they were always cold as ice. Most of the time those drink machines were located in a gas station and since there were no pop tops the bottle opener was built into the machine. If you could collect enough of those coca cola caps a Saturday morning kids show at the Bama Theater was yours to enjoy.

...Only girls wore earrings. A boy wouldn't be caught dead with the jewelry and no one ever wore just one except for Mr.

Clean. There was one exception to the earring rule – the boy's beauty walk, where guy after guy would priss around like a dolled up girl trying to walk from one side of the stage to the other without falling and breaking his fool neck in those clumsy high heels.

...Only sailors and Hell's Angels had tattoos. I take that back – kids could buy a tattoo patch and make their own that disappeared almost as quickly as it was applied. So if you saw someone with pictures on his body you could count on his being a navy man or a gang member or a little kid playing around.

...School always started the day after Labor Day. The warm-up for back to school was always the Labor Day parade which was a big, big event in our neighboring town of Tuscaloosa. Everybody in the county showed up and all the high school bands played in it. I would stand in the crowd, wave at my dad who was walking with all his paper mill buddies and other blue collar workers and then I'd wink at the pretty majorettes who made me realize why going back to school was a good thing.

...Nobody cursed in a movie except Clark Gable in "Gone with the Wind" and he even waited until the last scene to use the vile word. You could sit in the theater with your whole family and never have to be worried about being embarrassed by hearing words that your mother would slap you sideways for saying or seeing people parading around in their altogether like they were in their own bathroom at home. Today the movies have turned a whole nation into a Peeping Tom society.

...Eating out was a luxury. Mom was the only chef we knew and she fixed three meals a day. The only plastic involved was the wax paper on which she put the made from scratch dough to make the crust for our apple pie.

...You listened to the football game on the radio because only one game a week was televised. So you got to see your team play about once a season – if they were good enough to be on TV. Most teams weren't.

...Your TV only had two channels. So you only had three choices – channel 6 or channel 13 or go outside and play.

...When a third channel (33) was finally added you could only pick it up with rabbit ears that sat atop the TV. And even then you had to cover the wire with a piece of tin foil that you had to move up and down every time the picture went fuzzy. We kids were the first remotes as we took turns doing the foil job and changing the channels while Dad sat in his easy chair directing.

...If you missed the evening news at 5:30 you just missed the news for the day. If people had had to watch news around the clock back then they would have gone crazy. Which is the reason there are so many crazy people in our society today.

...The only underwear looking stuff women wore was in the bedroom, not on the streets. I think Madonna was the culprit who started the public underwear trend. Maybe just as Lady Godiva had to ride a horse through the streets naked Madonna should have to parade through the streets in her undies. But the only thing wrong with that idea is that she already does.

...Dizzy Dean and Pee Wee Reese were the only baseball announcers you got to hear. And they didn't care what your politics were as long as you enjoyed the game. I wish they could bring them back.

...Alabama didn't dominate the college football world. Oh, the Tide won an occasional national championship but the domination didn't happen until after I started shaving and wearing deodorant. When I was twelve years old I sat on my front porch and listened to the 1957 Alabama–Auburn game hoping against hope that Bama would pull it out. They didn't. They got beat 40-0 and Auburn went on to win the National Championship. However, a few years later along came this guy named Bear Bryant and changed everything.

...You were afraid of your teacher. Your teacher commanded respect and got it. In every showdown between teacher and student the teacher won. And for all our complaints, down deep inside we knew these people were doing us a favor trying to stuff some knowledge into those ignorant heads of ours.

...In every small town there was a place where all the teenagers hung out. Our place was The Patio where you could go and see everybody in town as well as chow down some of the best burgers anywhere. If you really wanted to be one of the "in" crowd you drove across the river to Jerry's Drive-in in the Rosedale area of Tuscaloosa. We guys and gals knew that if we didn't have anything else to do we could always go to Jerry's and drive around and around the place noticing and being noticed. It was fun. And sometimes we even bought something.

...If you caused trouble in school you could expect trouble at home. Which is why I almost never got into trouble in school and the one time I did I made sure my folks didn't know about it. I was in the fanny protection program.

...A little boy could go anywhere in my small town and be one hundred percent safe. It's as though everybody had been trained to look out for the other fellow and especially little kids. In fact, they really had been trained – by their moral teaching in church and home and at school and in society at large.

...In the winter your mom made you wear those awful wool pants. I had only one suit and it was made entirely of the wool material and scratched like crazy. It was okay when you were out in the cold but when the temperature climbed as it did when you sat next to the heater in your Sunday school class it was inhumane punishment for a little boy. That's why I never have worn a totally wool anything since then. This is in honor of all little boys everywhere.

This is the world I grew up in. This is the world I write about.

Pig Day, Fun Day

It was a big day. It was a pig day. It was a fun day. Actually, it was 4-H Club Day. And there I was standing behind the mark our leaders had drawn for us - on one side along the first base line were about a hundred boys and on the other side at the pitcher's mound was a little pig all greased and ready for action. Every boy had as his goal to catch that sty creature and win the coveted prize. And the pig's goal was to evade and make fools of all of us - which he did over and over most of the afternoon.

This congregation of crazies took place at the Queen City Park softball field down by the river on the Tuscaloosa side. But this day wasn't about softball – it was about pig chasing. The highlight event of the day was about to take place and every eager beaver boy was primed for action. I have to be honest and tell you that I really didn't want that pig (although I had already made arrangements for him up on my granddaddy's farm just in case). I only wanted to catch this little hog-to-be. My competitive spirit was stronger than it had ever been. I wanted to win. And I knew just how to do it – outrun every one of those other fellows who was giving chase.

Easier said than done. How could I ever outrun my fleet-footed classmates – guys like Bobby Sellers and Johnny Smalley? I didn't know if they were more powerful than a locomotive but I did know they were faster than a speeding bullet so I knew I couldn't keep up with them. What I needed was to somehow come up with an unknown factor. And I did.

Those who engage in warfare tell us that you have to get into the brain of your enemy if you are to defeat him. Well, I got to thinking – what if I go one better – what if I get the enemy's brain into me. Hey, now we're talking! That could be the deciding factor. So for breakfast every morning that week I dined on one of my dad's favorite dishes – pork brains - scrambled up with some hen eggs.

Now if that sounds too gross for you then all I can say is that you're just too squeamish for the wonderful delicacies of Southern cuisine. You'd probably faint dead away if you saw a plate of pickled pig's feet. And heaven help you if you had to bite into a chicken gizzard. My mom would understand that grossed out feeling which is why anytime we enjoyed this brain food Dad was the one donning the kitchen apron. I mean there are some things that even a mom is not going to do for her family. Okay, Mom was a trooper when it came to frying up those rodent- looking squirrels that Dad and I brought home but she drew the line short of pork brains.

And if that strategy about the pork brains sounds a little too foolish for you just remember that we're talking about a seventh grader here. Seventh grade boys are noted for leaping first and thinking later – if they think at all. I know. I used to be one. I remember my cousin Douglas telling me that the timber tall NBA star Wilt the Stilt Chamberlain grew to over seven feet by hanging on a chin-up bar. And I believed him. So for a few weeks there I couldn't pass a door without jumping up and hanging on it for a spell. Now you can understand my seventh grader pork brain logic.

Meanwhile, back at the softball field. As I said, we were primed and ready for the big pig chase. The air was electric with excitement in anticipation of what was about to happen. Everybody was in his fast-break stance when the gun sounded and what happened next can only be described as pig-demonium. That little lard-laden creature headed straight for center field (probably a Mickey Mantle fan) and then bolted left and rounded back to third base with wild-eyed kids hot on his little pigtail trail. Somewhere around home plate one of the boys lunged at this fast-moving target but all he got were a brief squeeze and a loud squeal from the slop-fed animal before that ham on legs headed out to centerfield again. That only served to excite us boys even more and once again we were off to the races.

Round and round we went with first one, then another diving and missing the visitor from the pig farm. Finally, with tongues hanging out and clothes as filthy as the pig we were chasing we were about to give up when one of the more durable guys grabbed him and held on. It was curtains for little Porky. This little piggy had come to the end of his rope. He threw in the towel! He called it quits! He said uncle! He raised the white flag! And a surprised little boy walked off with the prize cuddled up in his arms.

I don't remember what the rest of the guys did, but this little pig-chaser cried wee, wee, wee all the way home. It had been a ton of fun!

Thus begins my tale of fun-time living when I was a little boy growing up in a small town. It was such exciting fun that I thought

I would title this book "The Adventures of Growing Up in a Small Town", but I had a problem with that word adventure. Adventure means climbing Mt. Everest or swimming the English Channel or travelling across the Sahara Desert or trying to survive the Alaskan wilderness or sailing around the world or flying to the moon and back.

I love those on the edge of your seat stories of high drama. But growing up in a small town? I mean, it's fun and exciting and wonderful but it's not an activity that puts you in danger of falling into an ice crevice or going under the water for the third time or dying of thirst on a sand dune or being eaten by a Kodiak bear or turning your sailboat over and swimming with the sharks or being left in space to die out among the stars and planets far, far away from earth home.

So I did away with the adventure word and replaced it with the fun one because growing up in a small town is fun and a ton of it.

But first, fun has to have a place to happen. So let me introduce you to the little town that provided the setting for all this hilarity.

I

Welcome to My Hometown

The Choice of a Lifetime

BEFORE I WAS BORN I did something I highly recommend to all unborn children - scout around for a place where you can get the most out of growing up. My pre-birth question of the day was - should I spend my childhood in a small town or a big city? Well, just thinking about all that wall to wall traffic and more horn-blowing than a flock of geese heading south for the winter was more than my little unborn self could take so I opted for a quieter place – a place that gave you that out in the country feeling even when you were in the city. That's why I chose the little town of Northport, Alabama and I'm glad I did because when I was a kid Northport had it all. And according to the latest poll of me, myself and I it still does.

Of course, our little town has grown five-fold since I was a barefoot youngster roaming its neighborhoods, but some things have always stayed the same. The downtown area still consists of only one street with stores on both sides. You can't get any smaller

1

than that. Okay, I did drive through Repton, Alabama on my way to Florida one time and saw stores lining only one side of the street with nothing but a railroad track occupying the other side. And okay again, Northport does have a second street - a back street with a few more businesses – but if you drive down it you get the sensation that you're in somebody's driveway.

So a tour of our downtown is over as soon as it starts. But that's not going to stop me from pointing out a few of the more famous spots around here.

The Best Little Place to Feed Your Face

Let's say that you're an early morning fisherman who needs a hearty breakfast before heading to the old fishing hole. Or you're a businessman needing to carry a client out for a great lunch at an economical price. Or you're a University of Alabama student who is tired of pizza and tacos and you want a good home-cooked meal. Or you're a hungry husband who is in the dog house and whose wife is on kitchen strike. The answer to your need is the City Café located right in the middle of downtown – if such a small place can really have a middle.

I have to admit that I didn't eat at the City Café that much when I was a kid because they specialize in home-cooking and in those days my mom was home cooking. But sometimes Dad and I stopped by for an early morning breakfast before heading out to try to catch a few whoppers in the river or somebody's lake. And, of course, there have been many times since then when I have experienced the pleasure of eating at this famous Northport establishment and I have always come away deeply satisfied.

The City Cafe has been serving most of West Alabama since way back in 1931. That covers a lot of time and territory. And people. Even the late great Bear Bryant ate here. So did a lot of other noteworthy people. And some on the other end of the note spectrum. Just come in and look around and you'll see the rich and famous side by side with the poor and obscure. My crowd tended toward the obscure side.

Burt Reynolds and Sally Field - they're the famous ones. Jim Smith and Lester Loggins. You don't know them? They're the obscure ones. It's a very democratic place we have here.

Now before you take up that spoon and fork I can tell you this - your taste buds are in for a treat. Once you dig in those taste detectors are going to rise up and applaud like they've just heard a George Strait concert and your pocketbook is going to join in with more hearty amens than you'll hear at a Pentecostal revival meeting. That's because you're going to be eating some of the best home-cooked food at the lowest prices you'll find anywhere in the world. Well, maybe as a native Northportian I'm prejudiced, but I don't believe I'm too far off the mark.

Hey, don't take my word for it. Just witness the lunch-time crowds. My claim is easily backed up by all this mass of people standing in a long line waiting their turn to get into this place. I mean, at the noon hour it's a madhouse of activity since not only the local patrons drive in from all over Northport but half the students at the University of Alabama cross the river every day to dine on food that is sumptuous enough to compete with the mom-made dishes back home. And every once in awhile some ESPN announcer such as Todd Blackledge is going to sample these dishes and then go out of here bragging to the whole nation about what a feast he has enjoyed at Northport's City Café.

For years Joe Barger was the owner of this place and my claim to fame is that Joe and I were teenagers together. And when the two of us were boys old Tennessee Ernie Ford was belting out "Sixteen Tons" about how this guy started working in the coal mines the day he was born. I don't think Joe and I started working at the old Pure Process ice cream plant the day we made our appearance on this planet but we both started working in this world of creamy delights before our voices turned from alto to bass.

Back then as we were dipping our famous vanilla fudge ice cream and crushing ice in the old ice house that had to be the coldest place south of the North Pole we never thought that one day Joe would be the owner of the City Café and that I, along with thousands of other people, would be putting our feet under his table and eating his grub.

Of course, that didn't surprise me at all because I always knew that Joe was going places that a lot of guys only dream about. After all, he was a hard worker and somehow had more sense than the rest of us. Also, he was liked by boss and co-workers alike. The boss because he was a tireless and dependable worker. The co-workers because he always laughed at our stupid jokes. And let the record show – the things we teenage boys could come up with rated at the top of the stupid-o-meter.

At one time I worked in my sister-in-law's shoe store just across the street from the café and I had a daily routine which consisted of making my way over just before the lunch rush and ordering a slice of blueberry pie to go. I would bring it back to the store and sink my teeth into the best blueberry pie you've ever tasted and for the next several minutes I was in pie heaven savoring every delicious bite. Everything else was on hold until I finished.

Now get this picture. A lady walks in while I'm fully engaged in pie tasting. She walks up to me and says, "I'd like to look at a pair of comfortable loafers."

I look at her and reply, "Lady, can't you see that I'm eating pie and not just any pie but blueberry pie and not just any blueberry pie but blueberry pie from the City Café. So please don't interrupt me."

She replies to my reply, "Isn't it the business of a shoe store to sell shoes?"

I reply to her reply of my reply, "Listen, the reason I sell shoes is to make enough money to buy blueberry pie which I am now eating, so you'll just have to hold your horses until I get through."

Poof! Then I wake up. No lady customer. No blueberry pie. Just a dream that gives insight into my hungry soul. I'm living for Joe's blueberry pie. I'm even dreaming about it.

Not long ago I was in the City Café asking if they still serve the famous dessert. They don't. So here's a tip for anyone who wants to make some good money. Get Joe's recipe, set up a blueberry pie stand and get ready for the whole of West Alabama to rush in and do business with you. Hey, you'll make enough to get rich off of me alone.

You may be wondering why I don't do it myself. Simple. I'd rather eat blueberry pie than make money.

The Long, Long Train Trestle

If you leave the City Café and head toward the river (the Black Warrior River that separates our little Northport from big Tuscaloosa) and if you flick those eyes over to your right you'll see the longest wooden train trestle in the world. At least, that's what I've been told by reliable sources. And you know a reliable source wouldn't lie. We're proud of this landmark and I'm always bragging about it to people passing through.

My mind floats back to yesteryear. It's springtime and a young man's fancy turns to thoughts of…well, a railroad track. I'm a twelve year old kid walking this track with a bunch of my buddies. Give us enough time and the love fancy will become a big part of our thought process but today we're into rails and trains and trestles.

"Hey, have you guys ever walked all the way across the river on this trestle?" That, of course, would be a stupid thing to do since the trestle rises from almost ground level where we got on to a height of over a hundred feet by the time you get to the river. Nobody with any sense would even entertain the idea which is why someone in our group entertains the idea. When you're twelve you are all about adventure whether it makes sense or not. Which is why little boys are always getting into trouble.

"I don't think we should," says one of our gang. That would be me. I'm already getting a little dizzy-headed because of my fear of heights. That, coupled with the sudden insight that if we get to the river and a train heads toward us we would only have two options – plunge the hundred feet into the river or get run over by the massive

5

steel on wheels. And that causes me and some of the other guys to veto the suggestion.

Which shows that we are not totally stupid. There is a limit to our daredevil tendencies.

Which is also why we all will survive our kid years and become sane adults. Well, almost sane.

You'd think that all a train trestle would be good for is to transport trains. Or for little boys to walk on. Not so. Our trestle also makes an excellent background for photographs and that is what brings so many photographers – professional and amateur – out here to snap away. I've snapped a few pictures here myself. It's a very scenic place. I have a closet full of pictures of my granddaughters posing beside this old trestle. Beautiful young girls can make an ugly old thing look good. Which is why I'm always getting them to pose with me.

I've always had a fascination for railroads. Right across from my childhood home was an open field that ran right up to the track. Every kid ought to have the chance to live close to a railroad because it's a world of entertainment all in itself.

"Hey, Tommy, want to have some fun over at the railroad track?" I'm nine and Tommy Swartz is my seven year old neighbor and almost every day he'll meander over to my backyard for playtime. But today we leave the yard and walk across the field behind Tommy's house. It's about a football field's worth to the track and when we arrive I take out a penny and put it down on one of the rails.

Tommy looks over at me and asks, "What're you doing that for?"

I explain to him in kid language the dynamics of metallurgy. "That train's gonna flatten this penny."

You may think that a penny is already flat. That's because you've never seen an old Abe Lincoln that's been run over by a train. Now that's flat! So we wave at the engineer and I retrieve my flattened one cent piece and Tommy, wide-eyed with amazement, yells, "Wow!" I'm a hero, of course. I have performed magic in

Tommy's eyes. Well, maybe it's not up there with Houdini but it's kind of magic.

My stock in the neighborhood has also risen. Do you know what a flattened penny can bring on the kiddy market? A whole set of marbles. Or a sugar daddy that you can lick all day.

It's fun living next to a railroad. It's also sad. Many times I would lie awake at night listening to that old train whistle in the distance and get kind of a lonesome feeling all over my insides. I'd wonder – Where is that train going? What kind of people live there? Will I go there some day? And then the more philosophical questions – What is life all about? Where will I wind up? What will I be like when I grow up? Will I meet a girl? Will we marry and live happily ever after?

All that from a train whistle blowing in the distance on a cool and clear September night!

If It Exists, Anders Has It

We're back in the middle of town on the other side of the café. We're standing in front of Anders Hardware. The first time I walked into this store I wondered what had happened. Was there a tornado or did the employees have a hardware fight? Stuff was strewn all over the place in what seemed like a haphazard fashion. There seemed to be no rhyme or reason to the arrangement of the multitude of items in that store. Kind of like my bedroom.

However, every time I accompanied my dad to this establishment and observed the verbal exchange between my dad and the clerk I came to understand that in Anders, contrary to appearances, everything has its place and there is a place for everything. That was proved when Dad would ask for an item – sometimes a very hard to get item - and the clerk, without hesitation, would go right to it.

Now there are hardware stores and then there are hardware stores and then there is Anders. This place fascinated me as a kid and still does as an adult. It would pay a person to drive two hundred miles just to see this store. Maybe even three hundred.

"Son, I'm going up here to Lamb's Barber Shop and get my ears lowered," said my dad. Maybe some people think that's a funny way of saying he's getting a haircut but it's really quite accurate. The hair is down on your ears when you go in and up away from your ears when you come out. Ears lowered. No doubt about it.

"So what are you going to do while I'm in there?"

My inevitable answer, "I'm just gonna hang around in Anders." I knew that would be more fun than just about anything else I could do while waiting on my dad to do his downtown business. So I never minded waiting. And sometimes when me and my buddies walked the six blocks to town we'd wind up in Anders. They wanted to be fascinated too. We'd go in looking and touching and picking up stuff and quizzing each other on the uses for these items.

It was fun. A whole lot more fun than any video game I have ever played. Except for maybe Tomb Raider.

Even though this store was for people who were serious about farming or fixing up and even though I wasn't into any of these activities very much I had cause on special occasions to do business with the Anders people.

Special occasion one: boys trying to put a race car together and we need a whatchamacallit that nobody in the neighborhood seems to have. Off to Anders. Special occasion two: I'm trying to get the confounded toilet to toil. Need a part. Off to Anders. Special occasion three: I'm putting up a mailbox and need to dig a hole. A shovel won't do, I've got to have posthole diggers. And who has posthole diggers? Off to Anders.

After a while I came to a conclusion – if it exists, Anders has it.

"Hey, I need a left-hand ball-peen hammer."

"Do you want a rubber or a wood handle on that hammer?" The clerk wants to know. "Well, it doesn't matter. They're both over here beside this bin of nails."

"Are those sixpenny nails?"

"No, this is tenpenny. Sixpenny is over here by the horse collars."

"Horse collars? You don't happen to have a horse to go along with those collars, do you?"

I think I'm being funny and then the clerk turns and yells to the back of the store, "Hey, Roger, is that mule still tied up out back?"

"No, just sold it but we have a couple of Clydesdales coming in on Thursday."

I guess I'm exaggerating, but not much. I don't think I've ever been in that store and ask for some item and not gotten it. The variety of stuff between those walls is mind-boggling. Not long ago I was walking through that store again looking for anti-monkey butt powder - and there it was. I knew it would be. And now I get all my anti-monkey butt powder here.

As a matter of fact, I would venture to say that if you want a good education for your children, in addition to sending them to school, carry them to Anders Hardware, let them walk through the store from front to back asking, "What is this and what is it for?" I guarantee you that what they learn there will be more valuable than all that stuff they're exposed to in working on their PhD. And they'll have fun doing it.

Of course, I would really like to hear you explain to your kid what you do with anti-monkey butt powder.

As I said, if it exists, Anders has it.

Beverly Hills II

Remember that Andy Griffith episode where Andy, Opie and Aunt Bee take a trip out to Hollywood and wind up in Caesar Romero's front yard? And the maid comes out and snatches Mr. Romero's newspaper from them and asks these sightseers from North Carolina to please keep off the grass? I've been there. I've been to Beverly Hills - not in Hollywood, but in Northport. And I've stood in the yard of the famous – it didn't belong to Caesar Romero but to Leon Blackmon. And I didn't get run out of his yard - I got invited to run in.

Mr. Leon Blackmon had twin daughters, Warriene and Lauriene, which is why, I guess, I found myself in his front yard one day with about a dozen other guys. Maybe we were there because the girls were there but when Jody Jobson showed up with a football our first love expressed itself. You know how boys are about their sports. It takes priority over just about everything under the sun.

One time I attended a home wedding on New Year's Day and with all those bowl games being played we could hardly keep the groom focused on the wedding.

"Do you take this woman to be your lawfully wedded wife?"

"I'll answer that, preacher, right after I see if the Tide scores on this next play?"

I'm guessing they probably spent their honeymoon watching Bama beat somebody in the Sugar Bowl.

So here we guys were being true to our calling as we set about making a football field out of the Blackmon front yard

"Hey, see those hedges over there?" We all do. We have pretty good eyesight. "That's the goal line on that end. And the driveway can be the goal on the other end." Got to have sidelines. "How about that cluster of pine cones by the side of the house and the street on the other side?" We are all in agreement - a congenial bunch until the game starts. Boundaries established and we are at it. Crash, crunch, thud! Sounds of the game! Right here in Bellwood.

I'd like to tell you that the twins were watching from the sidelines shouting, "My hero" every time I scored a touchdown. But I'm probably wrong about that. On two counts – getting girl attention and scoring touchdowns. You know how age plays tricks on the mind and mine has been tricking me so much that I'm thinking of getting it a magician's license.

You may think I'm talking crazy – and I'm not past that – but for some reason I always equated Bellwood with that place of the rich and famous in California. I thought that if you lived in this little neighborhood you were somebody with a capital S.

Because the movers and shakers of our little town resided here.

Because it was a prestigious place.

Because I thought that one day if I worked hard and was successful I, too, could live in this lovely spot.

Not long ago I saw a house for sale here and although it didn't meet our space needs I was tempted to buy it. Love this place!

Bellwood is actually the oldest neighborhood in Northport. The reason I know that is because of a sign at the entrance that says "Northport's Oldest Neighborhood". They still have a lot of pride and rightly so.

"Hey guys, let's go to the community center." We're hanging out on our street looking for something to do and the big dance at the community center pops into someone's mind. There are no Fred Astaires in our group but we decide to go anyway and hang around outside to see who is with whom – kind of like red carpet night at the Oscars. To get there we walk right through Bellwood.

"Hey, anybody hungry? Let's go over to Archibald's and get some of that lip-smacking good barbeque." This famous spot has one of the best advertising schemes around – just let that tasty smoke rise up from those delicious ribs and up through the chimney where it can float around the neighborhood for awhile grabbing the attention of noses everywhere. It drives people crazy until they just have to drop in on Mr. Archibald and his mouth-watering food. I don't know at the times I was just driving by and before you know it wound up with barbeque sauce all over my face.

Today we boys from Fourteenth Street are his victims. No, the smoke doesn't travel the half-mile to my yard but the craving for pit cooked ribs smothered in that special sauce does. So off we go. And to get from our place to his place it's right through Bellwood.

"Hey, fellows, let's see if Celia Ann Mims is at home." I'm talking about one of the prettiest girls in school and she lived not too far from my house and although I would never walk up and knock on her door I'm not past sauntering by her house just to see if she and some other local beauties are hanging out in her front yard. And to get from my house to her house…well, you guessed it…it's the Bellwood route again.

You can see why I always felt that Bellwood was the center of our little town. It was certainly the center of my roaming and besides it was located just a few blocks from downtown and nestled between Main and Bridge Avenues, the two main streets in Northport. It seemed that to get from somewhere to anywhere else I usually had to travel through Bellwood.

And so it was that this little neighborhood became engraved in my mind as Northport's answer to that famous Beverly Hills place. I don't know that any tour buses filled with autograph seekers came rumbling through it but this was a special place and I was privileged to live just a few blocks away from this idyllic setting with the shady streets and beautiful yards and famous people.

Caesar Romero may not have lived here but some people who were famous to me surely did. I've already mentioned Mr. Leon Blackmon, who was the picture of success - always dressed to the nines and as distinguished looking a gentleman as anyone in Hollywood. Maybe right up there with Mr. Romero.

Mr. Blackmon owned a shoe store in downtown, a hub of activity all its own as guys went in to get all decked out in their penny loafers and men stopped by to get shod with those heavy work boots and women purchased their Sunday best high heels and teenage girls bought their rah-rahs to wear to school and yell, "Rah, rah!" The entrepreneur of this busy enterprise was definitely a man respected in the Northport community.

And then there were the Jobsons who lived one street right behind the Northport Elementary School. A lot of people in Northport knew Mr. Joe Jobson, another community and business leader but the Jobson names that I recognized were Jody and his little sister, Ann.

We used to kid Jody, "How can such an ugly guy have such a pretty sister?" You know how little boys can say such mean things, but it was all in fun, of course, because Jody wasn't ugly, although his sister was a little cutie-pie.

I actually fell in love with her one time when I went to a play she was in at the elementary school. I thought she was so squeezably cute. But I never squeezed her. I was in high school at the time and high school boys only squeezed high school girls. And I didn't even do that because I was so shy. A girl was lucky to just get a handshake from me. That hug stuff was still far in the future for this bashful boy.

Every little town has a noted family and in Northport my nomination for that honor would be the Faucetts. Maybe that's because when I was a boy everywhere I turned there was a Faucett. And some of them lived in and around Bellwood.

I saw them at school where day after day one of my favorite teachers, Mrs. Sarah Faucett, would greet me with a big inviting smile. Bless her heart, she helped me move up from ignoramus to whatever is right above ignoramus. And her daughter, the very pretty Sally, would greet me with another smile as I passed her in the hall on the way to class. Well, she didn't just smile at me, she smiled at everybody and I was a part of everybody. So I took it personally. I couldn't help but notice her because I was a professional noticer back then - trained and everything with outstanding credentials.

I also saw Faucetts at the gym because Tuesday and Friday nights would find me at the basketball games watching more Faucetts turn on. I'm talking about the Faucett boys - Omar, Tom and John Paul - who were running up and down the court doing all that basketball stuff - dribbling and scoring baskets and sweating a whole lot while I was in the stands yelling my fool head off. I loved it.

I saw Faucetts every time I went downtown. For about ninety years you couldn't walk through the heart of Northport without seeing a Faucett's store sign and for half of that time we have had some kind of connection with the establishment. That's because in the early days my wife, Margaret Ann, worked there putting herself through school and in the latter days she shopped there putting her husband through poverty. The Faucett family really owes us a lot for keeping them in business. I hope they realize that.

And I saw Faucetts in the halls of government. You can still see Sam Faucett hanging around downtown and sporting some of the loudest pants in Alabama. He has always impressed me, not because of his striped and polka dotted attire but because he started early on making his mark on the Northport community. Back in his younger days he served our little town as a member of the the city council and in other ways. And because of his philanthropy we have some things going on in the educational and social worlds that we wouldn't otherwise have.

I know I'm rattling on about the Faucetts and I'm not sure that all of them lived in Bellwood, but I do know that some of them did. And still do. And that's my point. I'm talking about a beautiful neighborhood and shady streets and influential families. Our Beverly Hills.

I still love to drive through this community and think about the old days when Bellwood was the center of Northport and some of the most influential people in our city lived here and it was host to some of the best football games I ever played. Those were great days.

If Only That Old School Could Talk

"Rising midst the golden cornfields, 'tis our alma mater true..." How many schools do you know that have a reference to corn in their most sacred song? Probably not many. I'm thinking zero. But my dear old TCHS once upon a time was located in the middle of a cornfield. Well, by the time I started there were only a few rows on the outer perimeter of the school. Later even that was gone to make way for our new track field. But way back when TCHS got started it was located right there in the middle of cornfield county. And after the corn was gone we students would be reminded of our heritage every time we sang our alma mater about the golden cornfields and the velvet blue.

From Bellwood I'm walking north a few blocks and now I'm standing in front of my old high school. Well, I'm standing in front of where it used to be. For some reason a few years ago some strong and sweaty men came in here with bulldozers and crowbars and tore it down and for years all that was left was an arch and a monument overlooking a few acres of empty land.

But now they're erecting a middle school in that place. I was hoping for another cornfield.

The new Tuscaloosa County High School is several miles up the road. Tearing down old structures and building them far away from the original site happens all the time. I know that. They call that progress and I suppose it is but to me it was still sad to drive by the old school place and see nothing but grass and a few bare spots for so long.

I long for the school to be close to downtown but the people in charge tell me that it was moved from the center of little Northport so they could put it at the center of big Northport. Meaning it's now in the middle of the school district – that our little town has grown north and we have to go where the people are and change with the times. I haven't gone out and measured it so I just take their word for it.

But I can tell you this – I don't care how many reasons there were for moving the school I still feel a tinge of sadness every time I pass this old spot. I mean it's hard to get used to something not being there when it was such a big part of your life for so long. Okay, I admit it. I'm one of those slobbery sentimental traditionalists. The only change I like is when the light bulbs go out.

I have to tell you something and I hope you don't think I'm crazy – after all, the last time the doctor gave me a mental health quiz I could still manage to repeat most of my name and almost all the days of the week – but when I drive by here I can still hear things. I do declare, I believe that old school bell is still ringing and those voices, all kinds of voices are talking - teachers saying, "Come to the board and conjugate the verb to be"; students warning their fellow classmates, "You better be prepared to discuss the Peloponnesian War – it's the first question on the exam"; coaches yelling, "Get that butt down and lunge into your man"; the principal

15

announcing over the intercom, "Will the student who parked in front of the lunchroom loading dock move it…NOW!!!"

It's not insanity that's my affliction – it's nostalgia. And in my case there is no cure for it.

I saw a movie the other night and when asked about her old high school the star couldn't remember anything. I found that hard to believe. Everybody remembers something about the old school days. I know I do.

My mind walks me in the front door past the office and down the hall to the first classroom where Miss Pool swiveled one too many times in her old merry-go-round chair and hit the floor with a mighty thud. Well, I guess it was mighty – she was not a little woman. Just thinking of that day makes me smile – which is better than I did back then. I laughed out loud. So did everybody. But only after Miss Pool looked up at us and realizing how funny it must have looked for a plus size teacher to hit the floor in front of her class said, "Okay, you can all laugh now." So we had her permission.

Then we had the job of getting her up which was not going to be easy because as one guy put it, "I don't know where to take hold." And I confess I don't know what happened next but somebody must have figured it out because the rest of my memories are of Miss Pool teaching her class in an upright position.

I sat in Miss Pool's class the day the world came to an end. Well, it was supposed to – at noon. That's what the guy had said and everybody was talking about it. Some self-proclaimed prophet somewhere had predicted that everything would disintegrate at the appointed hour.

I remember that day well. There we were, students and teacher, every eye focused on the clock as it ticked away toward the noon hour. Did we believe the world was going to end that day? Not really, but it was fun to talk about it and watch the anxious faces of the more impressionable as the time drew near.

Tick-tock-click, Tick-tock-click. You could hear those old clocks clicking and ticking all over school. And here these timepieces were inching toward the fateful hour.

Suddenly the room grew silent. One more tick…and the world… would disappear.

And then it happened! The clock struck twelve! A collective gasp came up from the class. Immediately everything went haywire. Everything went up in smoke. The school was totally obliterated. No more English class! No more school! No more anything!

Except me. I alone survived and given the task of rebuilding a new world.

Well, at least that's the way it went in my less than academic mind. Of course, in reality everything was still the same as it always was. On with English. On with that list of vocabulary words we had to learn by tomorrow! On with football practice that afternoon where I would get knocked around a few more times by fellows who were twice my size and who loved to run over us half-pints. But I was kind of glad that my world was still around. I would hate to have missed out on the rest of my life.

My mind continues the tour into the past. I'm now going down the hall to the library at the corner. Miss Mary Emma Barnes is putting up with a library full of students who have come today to do some…ahem…research. Students will be students and so this big room that is supposed to be a quiet place suddenly becomes a little noisy.

Miss Barnes raises her voice above the din and says, "I hear some talking." George Hunt leans over to me and a couple of other brilliant scholars and whispers, "That's because we're talking." We all giggle and act as though George has just uttered the funniest words to ever come out of the mouth of a ninth grader. We're impressed, but not Miss Barnes. In a flash she heads our way and gives us one of her famous memos to read. Well, it's better than getting kicked out. That'll come next.

We have been researching names for our fellow students. It's not enough for a guy to have a name, every fellow deserves a nickname. Early on Ronnie Fowler slapped me with "Gray Head" and Leroy Robertson gave George the "Tweety Bird" moniker. So we aren't bashful about labeling other guys. That one over there is Pug-nose

Pete. Ha-ha. And there is Moose. Ha-hee-ha. And that guy looks like Pickle-brain. Giggle, snort.

We're being silly, of course and you can tell that being kind is not one of our distinguishing traits. Neither is discernment – because pickle brain is actually a very smart and talented guy. Of course, we try to never call these people by their new names if they are bigger than we are. At least give us credit for that. We may be dumb but we are not stupid. We just giggle and snort like the silly and immature teenagers we are. Give us a few years and we'll grow up to be silly and immature adults still giggling and snorting about something just as inane.

"Mrs. Maxwell, what do you think about heaven?" My mind has now put me across the hall from the library and into Mrs. Bessie Maxwell's classroom. When you're a teenager you're inquisitive about a lot of things so we don't mind broaching a theological subject in a world history class.

And Mrs. Maxwell, who was one of my most favorite teachers, doesn't mind answering in her own unique way as she launches into a long monologue about the heavenly experience - how that when she gets to heaven she doesn't care about walking around on hard gold-paved streets in golden slippers. She explains, "That would hurt. What I want to do is kick off my shoes and walk barefoot though the grass. Don't you think that will be all right?" I don't shout "amen" but I think it. I like to walk barefoot through the grass, too.

Bless her heart, Mrs. Maxwell had a heart attack the year I was in her class and regardless of everyone thinking that we students had caused it I think it had more to do with her high cholesterol than anything else. I saw her downtown Northport a few days before she returned to the classroom and confessed, "We really do miss you." And I meant it. Like I said, she was one of my favorites and I dearly loved this woman. Even though her sub was a beautiful young woman named Miss Franks - which is why I went out of my way to show her the ropes, so to speak, and volunteered to stay after class every day and wash her blackboards. You know, just to be helpful.

My mind now leads me way down the hall and to the right into Mrs. Darden's room. She had her daily ritual, beginning every class session with the same series of questions. "Now, class, what is a noun? What is a verb? What is a preposition?" She knew the value of repetition so she kept it up until she had ingrained those eight parts of speech into us all.

Check us out. If you happen to run into an old County High alumnus stop and ask if he or she was lucky enough to have been in Mrs. Darden's English class and, if so, ask that former student to name the parts of speech. But don't ask me. As I told somebody not long ago the older I get the better my forgetter works.

But I haven't forgotten a lot of things that were said and done in that old schoolhouse. Hey, I have a whole section I want to share with you if you're still awake when you get to that part of the book.

The Big River

The Black Warrior River flows right between my hometown and the city of Tuscaloosa. If you're on the south side you're in Tuscaloosa. If you're on the north side you're in Northport. If you're in the middle of the river I don't know where you are. Most people around here call this body of water simply the Warrior River. And it played a big part in my childhood.

I look across the vacant lot into my neighbor's backyard where my friend, James Eads, is wearing cut-off blue jeans and carrying a cane pole. I know what that means. He is off to the river. He yells over to me, "Hey, Bill, want to catch a few whales?" I know what that means, too. He'll catch the whales and I'll catch the minnows.

James was always living some kind of adventure and one of the more frequent venues for those exciting times was down by the riverside. One day James came in from one of his fishing excursions and seeing me playing in my front yard beckoned, "Hey, Billy, come and look what I've got." And I did look – at the biggest catfish I'd ever laid eyes on swimming around in his bathtub. We didn't have an aquarium in the whole county so James' bathroom was the next best thing for displaying marine life. It was Sea World before there was a Sea World because from time to time there were other water critters in that reservoir. You can readily see that had it not been for James' tub I might have suffered some cultural deprivation. And that would have been very sad.

James was a Huckleberry Finn kind of guy who lived on the river because to him the only school he was interested in was a school of fish from which he could snag a few whoppers. After ten years of schooling James had had enough of the classroom scene so he said bye to the school and hello to the great outdoors. And that meant, more times than not, the old river bank.

Many times I'd join Huck for a day of fishing down by the Oliver Lock and Dam. We loved that place. The big river was quite different from those little creeks we usually hung around. It was nice to sit there and while away your time trying to hook a big old catfish but it was just as nice lazing around on the river bank and taking in all the sights and sounds of river life – tugs pushing their cargo down the river and the water spilling out over the dam and the birds chirping and the fish jumping. It was actually quite serene. Even when the big loads came floating by you could hardly hear anything but the gentle sound of the coal bins knifing their way through the water. Of course, the closer you got to the dam the louder the roar of the water. But even that just added to the serenity of the scene.

Our Black Warrior River was not only noted for fishing but also for flooding. I remember when the floodwaters from the Warrior would engulf downtown Northport and everybody would come down to see water, water everywhere. My dad would drive us to see the submerged area and pull up so close to the water that we kids would squeal with excitement, half afraid that he was going to drive the car into the watery mass and half afraid that he was going to drive away, but enjoying it so much because it was so cool.

We have a restaurant right on the river – the Cypress Inn - and if you look out the window you'll see a ladder of signs nailed all up and down one of the trees on the water's edge. Those are references to the depth of the flood waters and one of those is significant to me because I was right there in the middle of that flood. The waters hit 176 feet, way above flood stage, that year in 1979 when my sister-in-law had a shoe store in downtown Northport.

With the waters rising by the minute our whole family hustled to the store to rescue as many shoes as we could – getting some of them out of the store and into my brother-in-law's camper and moving the others to the top shelves where hopefully the water wouldn't reach. We began this rescue project wading around in ankle high water and by the time we finished it was up to our shoulders.

It was scary, racing against time and the rising waters and the threat of any water moccasin looking for a discounted pair of shoes. But it was exciting, too, and in a way it was fun. Although there was one tense moment when my wife got into a boat with a group of people only to discover that they were headed toward the river instead of back up to dry land. I was standing helplessly by seeing the love of my life slipping away into waterworld while yelling for someone to rescue her. I had left my superman outfit at home so I could only hope that someone who could leap tall buildings and rescue damsels in distress would hear her cry for help and would come and assist her.

And just as in the movies, someone did come to the rescue. His name wasn't Jim Dandy but this hero pulled his boat up beside her and with a mighty heave hoisted her up into the safety of the only boat heading toward dry land. That man of the hour was her brother.

It's a weird feeling to see the streets you drive on every day totally submerged in water. That used to happen all the time but now we are protected from such catastrophe by a system of locks and dams. And I'm glad. I'd just as soon leave waterworld to Kevin Costner.

The Old Drawbridge

Bridges fascinate me. I'm all the time googling the longest or highest or most dangerous bridges in the world. Well, I'm sure that none of our bridges connecting Northport with Tuscaloosa would qualify for google status. Except in my dreams. I'm talking about a recurring nightmare of our old bridge rising so far up into the sky that it gets lost in the clouds. And I'm trying to drive over it while my head is doing the swim job and my heart is beating like a drum in a Tarzan movie.

Okay, I admit that I'm afraid of heights, which probably contributes to my nightmare bridge travel. I lived in New Orleans for a time and just thinking of going across the sky-high bridge over the Mississippi River scared the wits out of me. And having no wits is not a pleasant thing.

For a long time there was only one bridge connecting Northport and Tuscaloosa and that bridge was a drawbridge that went up to let the boats go by and went down to let the cars pass over. There was a little room on top and it went up and down with the middle portion of the bridge and I think the guy who manned the controls delighted in stopping traffic at the most inconvenient times. Which led to a lot of impatient adults saying things that shouldn't be said and a lot of kids exclaiming, "Wow! Look at that!" as they sat wide-eyed in the car witnessing the magic of half the bridge moving up and down.

Sometimes, though, the fun was not riding, but walking, across the old drawbridge.

Four of us boys are taking a trip from Northport to Tuscaloosa and we know what that means -navigating this monster on foot.

"You ever walked across the bridge?" That's me taking a poll of who has and who hasn't. I've ridden across many times but walking close to the water is a different story.

"I have" says Terry Beck. Sure he has. He's the oldest and toughest among us. He's not afraid of anything. When he grows up he'll be a military man even putting in a stint with the FBI.

"I have" says Ronnie Davis. He's noted for doing anything – whether it makes sense or not. A little daredevil. I love this guy. He made my childhood fun.

"I've never walked across it but it's nothing but an old bridge. So I'm not afraid." That's Don Eads making that confident speech. We'll see.

"I've never walked across this one but I have walked from one side of the creek to the other on an old log down behind my house." I actually have but now I'm trying to be funny. Nervous and funny - cracking jokes and acting silly, hiding my anxiety.

We get to the bridge. Three of us start over without any hesitation but about a quarter of the way across we notice that Don is not with us.

"Hey, Don, you coming?"

Don doesn't answer. Something's wrong. His feet are frozen to the ground. And it isn't even wintertime. He's dead in his tracks. He can't move. He's just standing there like a little boy statue welcoming all those bridge travelers to the city of Tuscaloosa. Except this statue is not smiling.

Don motions for us to go on. His excitement for whatever is on the other side has dissipated. He only wants to put it in reverse and head home.

Nothing doing. We're not marines but we already live by the principle that you don't leave a buddy behind. We're all in this or nobody is in this. So we make a u-turn and for the next thirty minutes coax the future policeman across the big bad bridge.

But I don't think he ever had to chase a criminal across the river on foot. At least, I'm hoping he didn't.

The Black Warrior River and the old drawbridge. Fun place. Challenging place. I'm glad I grew up in a river town.

You can go to the Levee Restaurant on the Northport side of the river today and while devouring a big shrimp and catfish dinner you can look out the window and see the remnants of that old drawbridge. For somebody like me who over the years has driven and walked that bridge countless times it brings on a good time feeling and adds another reason I am glad I grew up in this little town of Northport.

Life under the Water Tank

Twenty-six fourteen, Fourteenth Street. Remember that address because it's a very famous place and one dear to my heart. It's famous because I lived here during my teen years. It's dear to my heart because I lived here during my teen years. But I didn't always live here. My home used to be a little farther west over behind the Holman Lumber Company. That means I had the rare privilege of living on both sides of a sawmill. Well, I'm not bragging, I'm just counting my blessings because these were some of the best times of my life.

Old Fourteenth Street is famous for another reason. It was home to another one of the town's landmarks – the city water tank, a giant structure that shot straight up into the sky.

And it was in my back yard. I thought it was one of the seven wonders of the world. Well, it was a wonder in my world.

Actually, there were two tanks – one concrete and one metal. So we got to double our pleasure. The concrete tank is still there covered with years of vine and tree growth making it difficult to see from the street. So if you want to drive by and see it now – which I'm sure will be high on your agenda once you have read this book - you'll have to slow down and really squint. And don't be surprised if people come over to your slow moving vehicle and want to know what you're doing.

"Hey, Buddy, what you staring at?"

"Well, I'm just trying to see that old water tank. Billy Gray says you have to really slow down and look hard to see it."

"Why in the world do you want to see an old useless water tank?"

"Billy says it's one of the seven wonders of the world."

"Hey, Louise, call the cops. We got another crazy one here."

Well, maybe it meant more to me than to anyone else. I loved having those giant water reservoirs in my backyard. Concrete tank for hard water and the newer metal model for soft water. You know I'm kidding. I just know they provided water for all of Northport.

Just think, all that water towering right over my house. I used to think that if the old tank were to spill over onto our humble little abode it would wash us all the way to the Warrior River.

Which is why I slept in my swim trunks and kept an inner tube by my bed. I wanted to be ready when the flood came.

Which is why I called myself Noah Junior. And named my inner tube "The Ark".

Of course, it never did wash us away but there were a few times when it did leak or overflow or something. Water would cascade down for several days until somebody from somewhere would come with a big wrench and fix it. Meanwhile, we kids had our own water park and we'd break out the cut-off blue jeans and jump in and out of the downpour splashing around and having the time of our lives.

Every once in awhile some guy would come out and climb up to the top to do his annual inspection of the tank and we kids would sit on the ground and watch him climb higher and higher until we got cricks in our necks making us have to look down at the ground for a spell. But it was fun – as fun as going to see a high-wire walker at the circus. And this was in my own backyard!

One day a man on the very top lost his footing and fell head-first off the tank to the ground below. But luckily, before reaching the old earth he turned right side up and floated on down unharmed. Oh, wait! That was in a movie I saw – "The Man with Nine Lives". It was part of a double feature with the "The Tomato that Ate New York".

In real life nothing that dramatic happened. Which I'm glad. I'd hate to see anyone fall from that height just as much as I'd hate to see a tomato eat New York. Washington D. C. maybe, but not New York.

Speaking of drama, there was this one time some of us boys thought it would be great fun to see how far up we could climb on that tank ladder. As it turned out, not very far. No sooner had we started our ascent than someone called us down. I don't exactly remember who it was but I do remember that he wore a badge and had a uniform.

Living under the water tank had certain advantages beyond watching the annual inspection show and enjoying the water park fun. Nobody had to search for my house. "Hey, Billy, where do you live?"

"Just look for the water tank and you're there." No street or house numbers. Just a big tank in my back yard.

Every once in awhile I'd run across a cocky kid who bragged about his swimming pool. "Ha, that's nothing. I have a water tank in my backyard that holds a zillion more gallons of water than your puny swimming pool and if you're nice to me the next time it leaks I'll invite you over for some real water splashing fun." Take that!

The Sawmill Community

I grew up in a sawmill community. Nobody in my family ever worked there but every day we heard the buzzing of the saw and the loud clapping of the freshly cut wood being stacked and the big whistle informing the workers when to be on the job and when to eat their lunch and when to go home. This beehive of activity took place at the Holman Lumber Company.

You might say that it was a little town within a little town because most of the workers lived in company owned houses surrounding the mill. And right in the middle of it all was a store where the workers and their families could buy most of what they needed and we kids could buy a ton of candy and gallons of coke and other assorted goodies.

We and several non mill workers lived right on the edge of that community and found ourselves falling into the rhythm of mill life.

6:55 in the morning: The warning to get that last wink of sleep. 7:00 sharp: Get out of that bed and start prepping for school. Noon: Didn't have to worry about this one during the school year but in the summertime this whistle meant we could start washing up for lunch. 4:00 in the afternoon: Time to stop messing around in the neighborhood and head home for homework and chores and the soon to be suppertime.

Actually, I lived on both sides of the mill – the country side and then later the city side. Our country abode was only fifty feet from the little bridge that marked the city limits, but that was enough for me to claim country boy status. And the reason that is vitally important is that I'm married to a woman who really did live way out in the country when she was a little girl – about fifteen miles from town up on highway 171 - and is constantly reminding me that I'm a city slicker and that she is the country one in the family.

I have to admit that Margaret Ann was an authentic country girl – even learned to milk a cow when she was only three. You know how it is - usually when company comes over proud parents will ask their kid to sing or play the piano or do somersaults for the people. But the Bigham folks herded their guests to the barn where little Margaret performed her cow milking ritual. I'm sure old Bessie groaned every time she looked up and saw that red-headed kid about to put her fingers you know where.

So my better half was a country gal, to be sure, but hold it there, sweetie. Just hold it, wife of mine, before you put me in the city dude category. I have you to know that my residence was once out in the sticks, too, with a little patch of woods bordering two sides of our house and a gravel road that went by our front yard. And for extra country boy points there was a huge pasture beyond our garden on the other side. And not only that but you could venture through the woods behind our house and find a little creek that was great for wading or seining for minnows.

Those woods, that gravel road and the garden and pasture land as far as the eye could see – well, you can just put me down for country boy.

27

And all this country living took place in sight of a sawmill.

But then for some unknown reason my dad decided to move us into the city – about six blocks away on fourteenth street – where I could look out on two water tanks and a chicken shack. I guess he wanted us to enjoy the finer things in life that only a metropolitan area can provide. So suddenly I was in a neighborhood with paved streets and houses up so close that when somebody sneezed the people in the next house yelled, "Gesundheit."

And kids everywhere - about a dozen boys my age - which provided me with a lot of fun and stories for this book. So pardon me if I mention from time to time Ronnie and Terry and Odis and David and Ronald and Donald and Roy and Jimmy and Donald Wayne and James and Don and sometimes Ronnie's uncle Terry and James' big brother Richard. And to pretty up the place let's throw in a few girls like Melna and Marcille and Donna Fay and Edna and Brenda and Sandra and Patricia and Elizabeth. Like I said…kids everywhere.

I remember those days fondly.

Both houses – city and country - were close enough to the mill that we could hear all that sawmill activity. And sometimes in the middle of the night we would all be awakened to a frightening sound – a series of short, loud toots from that whistle indicating an emergency at the mill and that all nearby workers needed to respond immediately. Our whole family would be roused from sleep, wonder what was going on down at the mill and sit on our front porch until the workers came streaming back to their homes with news that everything was under control.

That whistle sometimes messed with my mind. One hot summer night I went to bed with my windows open down toward the mill. It was a Sunday night and our pastor had delivered a rousing sermon on the second coming of Jesus. He told us about the end of time and the great shout and the trumpet that was so loud that it would wake up the dead.

All that was still weighing on my mind when suddenly that old mill whistle let out a series of loud toots indicating an emergency at the sawmill and all I could think was that Jesus was on his way. I know the Bible says a trumpet, but whistle or trumpet, it's all the same when you're an impressionable little boy with the second coming on your mind.

At one time the Holman Lumber Company fielded a baseball team. They practiced and played not far behind the lumberyard in sight of my country house and you could hear those pitchers popping that mitt a mile away. I'd sit on my back porch straining to see the game through my dime store field glasses and listening to the players pep talking each other – "Hey now hey now hey now" - and hearing a roar coming up from the crowd when somebody had just done something great. And I remember listening to my neighbors after the game talk about how some of these guys were good enough to play in the pros. As Yogi Berra used to say – you can observe a lot just by watching. So I observed. I watched. But more than that - I listened. Whiz pop! And then the roar of the crowd!

II

In and Around Town

If You Ain't City then You Gotta Be Country

IF YOU GO UP into the mountains of West Virginia and Kentucky you will hear about the famous Hatfield – McCoy feud. Stories have been told and movies made concerning that rivalry, but there are other people in other places where the rivalry is just as intense. I guess every place on the planet has a rival and that was no less true for our Tuscaloosa County High School. We Wildcats were on the Northport side of the river and our nemesis was that institution on the other side – the big town school, the Tuscaloosa High Black Bears. So anytime we took to the field or gymnasium or baseball diamond it was Cats versus Bears. And I can tell you this – our rivalry was Hatfield-McCoy all over again.

Well, without the killing.

Although sometimes the name calling escalated into full blown fistfights.

I'm ashamed to admit that I was a part of the name calling but I'm proud to say that I avoided the fist fight. Not that I was above fighting — I just knew that if I got into a fight over a ball game I'd probably get a licking — at the fight scene and then at home when my parents found out. My fanny was as tough as anybody's, but I didn't think it could bear up to a double licking on the same night.

We called those guys across the river City High and I guess logic compelled them to go with the opposite of city and call us Country High. And I suppose that made sense but being called country upset some people on my side of the river. I never could understand why because I was always like L'il Abner, the country bumpkin from Dogpatch, when accused of being a male chauvinist, replied, "Where is the insult in that?"

I didn't consider an accusation of being country something that needed to be denied. It never did bother me, I guess, because country flows through my veins and manifests itself in various ways. For one thing, I talk country — just ask anyone who has had the pleasure of hearing me rattle on about something and they'll declare that they've been listening to Farmer Brown. Or, in my case, Farmer Gray.

One time up in Huntsville I shared the platform with a South African preacher and when it was my turn to speak I said, "You've just heard a British accent, now adjust your ears because you're about to listen to one from the Heart of Dixie." Everybody in the audience laughed and seemed to accept me just like I was a regular human being - with a brain and everything.

And I remember the story about Elizabeth Maxwell, a brilliant TCHS alumna, going up North to med school (I believe it was Johns Hopkins) and thought she was really making a good impression because everywhere she went people asked her all these questions. She thought they wanted to hear what she had to say until it dawned on her that they just wanted to hear that Alabama accent.

Well, my accent betrays me, too. I'm from the South. I'm from Alabama. And more specifically, I'm from Country High. So there!

Another country attribute - I like country music. Well, most of it. My favorites go way back. Ernest Tubb, Hank Locklin, Faron Young, Roy Clark, Patsy Cline, Loretta Lynn, Marty Robbins and

Buck Owens (I don't know most of the current stars except those who have been around forever). I still go around singing "I Miss You Already and You're Not Even Gone", "Please Help Me I'm Falling", "Crazy" and all those pathetic songs about how to survive after being two-timed by your favorite gal who happens to be your sister's best friend. You know, that kind of stuff.

Like Barbara Mandrell sang – I was country before country was cool.

And one more thing that makes me proud to be associated with the country side of life – I think the smartest people on the planet live in the great outdoors next to nature. I distrust anybody who has never seen a cow in person. Or heard a rooster crow in the early morning. The bottom line is that I love country – well, all my people have country roots so how could I not.

I know there's irony here because I've been a city boy all my life (except for those few years we lived fifty feet outside the city limits), but the country has always been a part of me. My mom and dad grew up on a farm in the Mount Olive area of north Tuscaloosa County and a lot of the farm stuff they grew up doing I grew up doing also - hoeing the garden and plowing the field and planting the seed and whacking back those ornery weeds that try to take over and cutting that okra in the hot summertime while you're stinging and sweating to beat sixty and pulling that corn until your arm is about to ache off. And knowing what a great treat a big jug of ice cold lemonade is.

So what I'm saying is that I never lost sleep over what those city dudes called us. I was proud to be a part of Country High.

Now in saying this I'm not denying that those city slickers have a lot to be proud of, too. No sir. If I travel out of state and someone asks me where I'm from and if I say Northport they just look at me with a blank stare – like they want to ask "Is that in this universe?" So I just tell them that I'm from that little town across the river from Tuscaloosa and when I say that they always light up and say, "Oh, yes. Tuscaloosa. That's the home of the Crimson Tide." And the words "Crimson Tide" trigger an automatic reflex that catapults me out of my chair waving my arms and giving them my best "Roll Tide Roll"!

So I don't mind being associated with Tuscaloosa because truth be told, they've got a lot of things going for them over there on that side of the river. They have a public library. That counts for something. I love to read. And they have a mall. That counts for something, too. At least my wife thinks so. She loves to shop. That's where I take her on those days when I sense that she's depressed and needs a shop lift.

So, yes, there's a lot of pride in Tuscaloosa and I go along with most of it until you get to the high school rivalries.

T High (another name for them) was our biggest enemy when it came to sporting events. We guys and gals from the county school would cross the river and as soon as we walked into City High's gym their fans would be standing in those bleachers chanting "Go back, go back, go back across the river" and then they'd raise it up another notch with shouts of "River rats!" This verbal assault didn't bother us because we knew that when they came to our place we'd return the ugly favor. Of course, some of the more insane fans among us would take it personally and wind up in a scuffle or two in the bleachers. And instead of enjoying the game inside the gym they experienced the handcuffed life inside the police car.

You can readily see that there was no love lost between these two schools.

That's why it hurt so much whenever we lost to those guys. You see, we country people always believe that country boys are tougher than city boys so naturally we have to come out on top in a physical struggle. That's just the way life is supposed to be. But we didn't. Most times we came out on the short end and I couldn't understand that. Neither could my mom. She puzzled over it. "I thought country boys were supposed to be tough" she would say after every defeat.

"They are, Mom" I would assure her while searching for some explanation. "I guess our guys have just been eating too many of those cathead biscuits smothered with gravy and piled high with all that bacon and sopping up that ribbon cane syrup we're famous for over here on this side of the river. That and not plowing enough rows these days. That'll make a fellow weak. But we'll get'em next year."

Well, next year came and we didn't get'em. I think we lost to those city boys for something like twenty years in a row. But that didn't keep us from getting our hopes up every year. At every pep rally preceding the big game we'd work up to a fever pitch. My senior year Sonny Booth gave the pep talk ending in a rousing yell, "Go, big blue!" But big blue didn't go. We came close – closer than other years losing by a close 13-0 margin.

I thought our great 1960 team would surely get the upper hand. Nope. Lower hand again. We got smacked 33-7.

Now that defeat was really hard for me to understand because our team was sporting one of the best records in the state and had already beaten some pretty tough competition. Plus we had one of the best coaches around - Hootie Ingram - and we were loaded with talent.

We had such guys as Clark Boler – who was 6'5" the day he was born - and who was a star in every sport for four years and who went on to play at Bama and became one of Bear Bryant's favorites for his spirit and hustle. Then there was Buster Sullivan, a big bruising halfback and multi-talented athlete who took the ball up the middle and down the throats of many an opponent. And who could forget the wide load Mandeville Christian and quick as a cat Herman Parker who could open up a hole in the line big enough to drive an eighteen wheeler through. And our star QB was Roy Kelly who could not only throw it downfield but do it left-handed! I've tried that and it ain't easy.

Oh well, I guess some things are just not meant to be understood. The bottom line is that we were talented, but we lost. And the only conclusion I can draw is that we lost because we just didn't score as many points as they did. I know, I know. That's not much of an explanation, but it's the only one I can come up with. Otherwise, it is inexplicable – which is a word that I learned at Country High.

He Didn't Give Us the Big Head,
He Gave Us the Flat Head

When I was a kid I hated going to the barber shop. I guess all little boys do. I didn't mind actually getting my hair cut, it was the waiting that killed me. You know how restless little boys can be. We hated sitting there for a spell when we could be out chasing a baseball or one another or holing up in our secret hideout while plotting to take over the world. But there was one thing I always liked about waiting my turn at Lamb's Barber Shop – watching Mr. Hickman work a head. He was definitely an artist – a flat-top artist.

Not that he cut my hair. Walter Snider did the honors on my head. After all, he was kin to me. I think. My mother's sister's husband's uncle's sister's husband...or something like that. So naturally my kinship loyalty kicked in whenever I visited the old barber shop.

Still, I loved to see Mr. H work. He buzzed and snipped and looked and measured until his customer's hair looked as flat as a pancake. But that wasn't good enough for the flat top man. The young boys were never dismissed from the barber's chair until Mr. H laid his comb across the top of the mop making sure his comb sat there level all the way across the boy's flat head touching every hair equally. If it didn't pass the comb test the hair job wasn't finished

I always envied those guys who exited Mr. H's chair with the flattest top on the roundest head. It was cool! But, as I said, I was loyal to my kin. I liked Walter and he always picked at me and told me the funniest jokes while mowing my hair.

However, there was this one rare time when Walter was busy and Mr. H had just finished his last head. I guess Walter could see it in my eyes – this desire to have my hair cut by "the flat-top artist". So looking over at me and nodding, Walter said, "Billy, it's okay to let Hickman cut your hair today if you are in a hurry."

Was I in a hurry? You're always in a hurry waiting in the barber shop when you're a kid and not one of those old-timers who show up just to air out whatever they want to air out – sports, politics, weather, religion – you name it. These guys seem to be quite conversant on a number of issues. As a matter of fact the barbershop was where I got my second education. That's the reason I know so much useless stuff.

I leaped into Mr. H's chair with a feeling of expectancy and exultation at the same time and soon I could feel the buzz-a-buzz and snippity snip as the sculpting began. I couldn't wait to see the finished product on my punkin' head, as Snuffy Smith sometimes says. Then came the big moment – the comb test. I could sense every hair on my head pleading, "Please let the comb touch me." It did. That comb lay flat across every hair on my head or my name isn't... whatever my name is. I was elated! For weeks I walked around with pride showing off that flat head everywhere I went.

I had been to the flat-top artist. And today I count myself among the Hickman alumni. And I'm thinking that we ought to have a flat-top reunion or something. But I suppose that would be impossible because so many of these guys no longer have enough hair to flatten.

Agony and Ecstasy at Smith's Creek

Is it appropriate to sing "Shall We Gather at the River" standing on a creek bank? Well, appropriate or not, we did it. I'm talking about out little congregation of Five Points Baptist Church back in the 1950s. Our church actually had a baptistery – it was right under the pulpit – but our pastor, Brother David W. Lewis, liked to baptize people in the great outdoors when the weather permitted. Maybe he thought it was more authentic that way – kind of like John the Baptist baptizing Jesus in the muddy Jordan. And this baptizing always took place at Smith's Creek in the Flatwoods area.

Smith's Creek was quite famous around Northport. It was a multi-purpose area with the creek serving as a watering place for the cows, a fishing hole for us boys, a swimming pool for the community and a baptistery for the church. And the pasture land doubled as a grazing place for the cows and a venue for Sunday afternoon football for us community sports nuts.

More than once we guys would grab our cane poles and a can of worms or sometimes a jug of minnows and head out to the creek for a fun day of wetting a few hooks. Which is about all I did. When I baited that hook with one of those slippery minnows and threw it into the water all that was accomplished was that the little fishy got to say hello to all his under-water buddies.

Bunky Williams, on the other hand, would come back from the creek with a whole string of picture worthy whoppers. Same creek, Same bait. Same type of fishing gear – a simple cane pole. But a different result. Of course, that might have been because Bunky knew what he was doing and I didn't. But I don't think I want to get into that. I have too much respect for my mama who always thought I could do anything.

One of my most painful yet fondest memories is of a day of swimming at the creek. It was painful because someone had put up an old diving board full of splinters and I got one under my big toenail. That's where the pain comes in. It hurt. Like crazy. I wanted to cry but there were girls around and I didn't want to appear less than macho. So tears were out of the question. But I did moan a lot.

Horace Sexton did the surgery. He had brought me to the swimming hole that day and I guess felt somewhat responsible for my plight. Horace didn't have a doctor's degree but he did have a pocket knife and a match. So he lit the match and held it under the knife to sterilize it and began cutting. Here's where the fondest part of the memory comes in. All the girls in the swimming hole got out and came over to see how I was doing.

Horace told me to grab something and hold on tight while he cut away. I looked over at Ladye Miles and she said, "I don't think he means me."

By the way, Ladye's real name was Evie but somewhere she picked up the nickname, I guess, because this Ladye was a real lady and was liked by everybody. I know I did. I grew up and went from being her little boy neighbor to being her adult pastor. And she grew up and married Jimmy Mills thus becoming a part of one of the best families I've ever known.

All those years that Ladye and I were kids I had the idea that Ladye was the name she was born with and I kept quiet about it since I figured that it was none of my business anyway and besides if Tarzan could name his son Boy, Mr. and Mrs. Miles could name their daughter Ladye. Just to add to the fun she had a brother who was named Pot. I was grown before I knew his real name was Charles but, again, that's none of my business. I liked Pot, too. And the rest of this Miles family who lived down the hill from us and whom I saw often.

But back to the story at hand. As I lay there on the creek bank moaning and groaning the girls surrounded me with all kinds of sympathetic words and gestures. Linda Cabiness even held my hand. Which didn't help because then my blood pressure shot up. But I didn't care. How many times does a boy get to be surrounded by beautiful girls in swimsuits? Nobody I know except Elvis in that movie "Girl Happy."

Dr. Horace got the splinter out. And with that operation done the girls left my side and went back to swimming. I looked around. Hmmm…I wonder if there's another splinter in that diving board?

Things Backwards

I was standing on our back porch when I noticed a car creeping up our tree lined driveway. Those trees had been there a long time – survived wind and rain and hail and lightning. And my sister. She assaulted them when she was a mere fifteen and a half year old learning to drive. Dad had warned her about them. "Honey, make sure you don't hit those trees. Be careful about those trees. Watch those trees."

And she did. Hit every one of them as she breezed from point A to point B.

Dad shot out of the car and headed toward point C. Which stands for coffee. Which he needed right about then. Something black and strong and soothing. Sis survived the tree crunching and Dad's ire and went on to get her license. And today she drives and talks at the same time happily shuttling grandkids and assorted friends around the big city of Huntsville. And as far as I know she hasn't hit a tree since then. Scared a few pedestrians, but no tree damage. I'm so proud of her.

So here's this car coming oh so slowly up the driveway into our front yard. And before he can exit the vehicle I yell, "Drive on around to the front!" I'm not a mind reader but what's coming over the teletype in my brain has the man thinking, "Did that kid say come around to the front? I'm in the front!" And he was – sort of. He was in our gravelly front yard which faced our back porch and I wanted him to pull around to our grassy back yard which faced our front porch. What's so complicated about that?

A few years later, after we had moved a few blocks away, Ronnie Davis and I were riding our bikes around the old home place. We parked in the front yard and Ronnie exclaimed, "Hey, this is crazy! The back porch is in the front yard and the front porch is in the back yard!"

I explained, "That's because a tornado came through and blew the house all the way around." Ronnie wasn't buying it. He was a pretty smart fellow. So I told him the truth, "Actually an earthquake shook the ground so much that the yards switched places." He wasn't buying that either. He was still pretty smart and as far as I know he's still got all his smarts to this very day.

Of course, the real truth is that the house used to sit with the front in the front and the back in the back like most houses and then somebody decided that the road was all wrong and so they dug out a new route that put our front in the back and the back in the front. Any further questions?

So our house is an interesting conversation piece.

So is the Northport Methodist Church. It's backwards, too. I discovered that when I joined Polly Lindsey, Cary Christian and Larry Lawrence for a presentation to the church. We were all members of the Northport Elementary 4-H Club and what we did I have no idea but I know that we did something because somewhere in my closet I have a picture documenting the occasion.

I'm standing next to Polly who at the time stood a head taller than me. You might say I looked up to her. And I really did because all through elementary and high school I thought she was one of the neatest people on this planet and I loved being around her. She was beautiful and smart and a whole lot of fun and is still living somewhere in the state of Alabama, no doubt impressing other kids and causing other little boys to fall in love with her. Well, I didn't actually fall in love with her – I just loved the person she was.

Okay, that's my tribute to Polly Lindsey.

Back to the backwards church. In most churches when you enter the front door off the street you're standing in the back of the auditorium where a guy can adjust his tie or a lady can smooth out the wrinkles in her dress or a mom can give one last swipe across the little one's snotty nose. But in this church as you come through those doors you're suddenly staring everybody in the face where the whole congregation can witness first-hand those necessary last minute adjustments.

"Surprise! You're live and on camera from the Methodist Church in downtown Northport!" That's the feeling you get.

I went home that day scratching my head wondering why those Methodists built their church with the front in the back and the back in the front. I was used to that sort of stuff, of course, because as I have already pointed out I lived in such a backwards house. But I've pondered it a lot over the years and have come to a conclusion. Those Methodists are geniuses. They're very friendly people who want to get to know the people who visit them so they just designed a church where it's impossible for anybody to sneak in and out before they get a chance to say, "Howdy! How are you? Great to have you with us today!"

They've really thought this through. Here we Baptists are trying all sorts of ways to get to know our guests while the Methodists have figured out how to guarantee that a guest will never go unnoticed. Just switch the front and back.

So the next time someone says, "You folks here are really backwards" just smile and say, "Thank you."

III

Across the River

Saturday Morning Shootout

BULLETS ARE PEPPERING DOWN on the little band of people who have been making their way across the plains of Oklahoma. They're in the valley trying to take refuge in their covered wagon as the bad guys – with their black hats, of course – are perched on the rocks above shooting at the frightened travelers below. It looks hopeless for these lonely pioneers as they face off against this gang of assorted criminals – murderers and horse thieves and bank robbers.

With only enough ammo for one more round these desperate people still cling to the hope that one of their party has reached the fort and will be bringing reinforcements any time now.

But it doesn't look good.

Finally, the last shots are fired and the murderous gang descends upon the little remnant. This is the moment the good guys have dreaded. It is over! This is the end!

But wait! What is this? Suddenly… in the distance… a bugle sounds. And now the thundering sound of hundreds of hoofbeats.

The horses are running! The soldiers are riding! The Cavalry has arrived! Uncle Sam to the rescue!

And as the US Army comes roaring in, the Bama Theater erupts with yells and whistles and applause as kids all over the auditorium are standing in their seats slapping each other on the back and dispensing high fives to everybody within reach of their flailing hands. Every girl and boy is jumping for joy as if they've been right there side by side with those pioneers through it all.

Such is the magic of the big screen. Such is the thrill of Saturday morning kid time at the Bama Theater.

I am one of those kids. We have come from all across the county to watch this big show – sometimes a western with Roy Rogers and Dale Evans and Gene Autry and Randolph Scott and of course, the U. S. Cavalry; sometimes cartoons with Bugs Bunny and Elmer Fudd and Daffy Duck and Foghorn, I say, Foghorn Leghorn; sometimes Captain Marvel, that noted fighter of evil who said the magic "shazam" long before Gomer Pyle ever uttered the word; sometimes the muscled-up Tarzan and the shapely Jane and of course, the ever entertaining Cheetah. We take it all in and we'll do it again the next Saturday morning and the next and the next.

This is the way we and several hundred other kids spend our Saturday mornings. Our moms have sent us here so that for a couple of hours they can experience the serenity of a home without whining young'uns crying, "Momma, make Billy quit hitting me" and muddy feet tracking through the newly cleaned living room and little sisters running into the house yelling, "Brother just fell out of the tree and I don't think he's breathing."

Our moms know that it won't cost much for us to get in but are okay with whatever the fare as long as they can just get some peace and quiet for a short spell. More than likely we won't have to spend any money at all. Sometimes the entrance fee is a bunch of bottle caps or a used toy or maybe some candy wrappers – the fare is different each week. And when they do charge actual money and we guys arrive penniless we get innovative.

"Okay, it's going to cost us a nickel to get in. Any of you guys have any money?" Mickey looks at me and I look at him and we both look at Harold. We're as broke as a Saturday night gambler on Sunday morning.

"You know what to do", says the Mick. So ditching Plan A – which was arriving with money in our pockets - we spread out eyeing every nook and cranny of the area around the theater looking for some change that just may have dropped out of some unsuspecting man's pocket. That's plan B. Coming up empty we move on to plan C which is hitting all the phone booths feeling around for any coins that some absent-minded person left in the change receptacle.

"Nothing there. What's next boss?" We love to act like we're a gang of hoodlums. And sometimes there is no acting involved. One is the boss, one is the muscle and one is the lookout. I don't remember who was who but we all understand it's time for Plan D. We've been here many times before.

Mickey looks at me and asks, "Have you got it?" And with a nod I pull out a string and three pieces of bubble gum. We all start chewing. When the Joe Palooka gum is soft and flexible we kneel down on top of a sidewalk grate and like a skilled surgeon guiding a scalpel the steady handed among us attaches the gum to one end of the string and slowly lowers it to the bottom - a bottom that just happens to have a quarter and two dimes. The lookout had spotted them while we were in Plan C mode and had filed it away for future reference in case it became necessary to implement Plan D. It has now become necessary.

The surgeon boy maneuvers the gum-laden string until it lands flat on top of the big coin.

Everybody in the gang is smiling but breathing lightly. The crucial do or die part still has to be done. The doc boy draws a deep breath and then lifts the string ever so carefully pulling and pulling and pulling until the quarter is through the grate and into the hands of the steady one. He's a hero.

But the back-slapping is postponed. There are two more coins down there. So we pray. We hope. We watch as the hero does it two more times. And when he is done we all break out into the best back-slapping moment since we did this a week ago.

With money in the pocket the hero and his gang of admirers march around to the front of the Bama, pay our fare and speed on over to the refreshment stand where the hero yells, "Coke and popcorn for all my men!"

We fellows don't know it, but we've just confirmed an old saying – necessity is the mother of invention. And another old saying – to the victor belong the spoils. And one more – a good time was had by all.

Meeting our pals from here and there. Fishing for coins below the sidewalk. Watching movies in which you can tell the heroes from the villains. Guzzling coke and munching on popcorn. When you're a kid it doesn't get any better than this.

Over the River and through the Fair

Even though I enjoyed being a student and had a positive attitude about school I still looked forward, as any one-hundred percent All-American boy did, to every opportunity to miss being there when the old school bell rang. Such as Fair Day.

When I was a kid the County Fair was big – really big. All the schools turned out early for the event and just about everybody in the school showed up. There was nothing like the smell of sawdust and the taste of cotton candy and the thrill of riding the big Ferris wheel. Back then the County Fair was always held at the Jaycee Park in the part of Tuscaloosa that is called Alberta City which is located about a mile east of the University of Alabama campus. Cars parked everywhere – in the fields, up and down all the streets, in the Alberta churches' parking lots and if you were lucky, inside the fairgrounds.

"Okay, children. Wait up." Mom was trying to calm us kids down because it's not every day that you get to go to something this big and fun and exciting and we couldn't wait to hop on those rides that turn you upside down and sideways at the same time.

As soon as we got through the gate we were ready to hit the fun stuff. Mom wanted us to do the educational stuff. That's what makes a mom a mom.

So as fidgety as we were, we walked slowly through the display tents looking to see who had the best pickles and jellies and jams and who had crocheted the prettiest "Home Sweet Home" picture. "After all" Mom said, "there are students who have worked hard all year to excel in something other than reading, 'riting and 'rithmetic and I want you to take notice of that and see who has won a prize in what. Maybe you'll see what some of your classmates have done."

She was right. Moms usually are. I knew that Joe Doug Billings would always be in the running for raising the best cow or pig or rooster or something having to do with the farm. I think even his little sister won a first place ribbon one year. That's the way it works a lot of the time - farming gets in the blood and spreads to everybody in the family and stays there for generations. So Joe Doug takes the farm honors this year, Mary Ann will go home with the ribbon a few years later and their older brother Albert took top honors some time ago. Which is why if you want to know anything about raising cattle or crops ask a Billings. Moo and oink and cock-a-doodle-do, I'm sure, were music to their ears.

Finally, finally, finally we get to the midway where all the action is. I'm ready to get on one of those rides that puts your bottom on the top and your top on the bottom and swings you so fast and hard that you think you'll wind up in outer space. They even have a ride this year that lets you stand up while that machine is twisting you six ways to Sunday. They say ride it at your own risk. Ride it if you don't value your life. Ride it if you want to live as if there is no tomorrow. So I ride it. Then I get off and go around the corner, throw up and hop on again. The ad is right – there is no tomorrow. There is only now – and it's as fun as fun can be.

This is what every little boy longs for. And this is what every big boy longs for. With this difference – the little fellow goes solo, the big fellow goes duet. Meaning there is a gal attached to his side while the ride is tossing their topsy turvy bodies over against each other. Which gives a new meaning to "Hello there!"

Of course, you can't go to the fair without stopping by the games. But you have to be careful. Here is our pastor's son and me walking slowly through the midway trying to decide on what to play. I am about to learn a very important lesson at the expense of my friend David. He has five dollars in his pocket just waiting to be spent. We stop at a booth and I don't remember if it involved shooting a gun at some ducks or throwing a ball at some bowling pins, but David yields to the hawker's appeal to come on over and win a prize.

My friend puts down his quarter and takes a shot in the confidence that he'll win on the first try. Not bad to win a nice prize for a quarter. But it is misplaced confidence. Missed shots, no win, no prize. Another quarter. Same result. Five dollars worth of quarters later and still no prize. Why he kept on going I'll never know. He should have done as I did and spent most of his money on hot dogs, popcorn and cokes and rides before he ever got to the games.

Here's the lesson I learned – it's easy to get sucked into spending a lot of money in the hopes of winning a prize. I see it all the time in these casino ads. They never show the losers. It's like one of my friends said about betting on the horses. He quit when he noticed that there were twenty windows to place your bets but only one to collect your payoff.

David made me promise that I wouldn't tell anybody about his misfortune. And I haven't until now. But I figure that it's okay to go public now that he lives out of town and that was so long ago. And if you just keep your mouth shut and not snitch, we'll all be okay.

I went to the County Fair every year – as a little boy with my parents, as a big boy with my guy and gal friends and as a grown man with my wife. Fair days were fun days. Well, mostly.

On one particular occasion I was going through the fairgrounds with my neighborhood buddies Don Eads and Ronnie Davis. We shared a sense of adventure and did a lot of things together so when the fair hit town we hit the fair.

Ronnie wandered off somewhere to a ride or concession stand and left Don and me standing in front of the haunted house. We stood there for awhile listening to the blood-curdling screams emanating from the inside and trying to decide if we wanted to enter the spook show and get scared out of our wits. Since we didn't have much to lose we bought our ticket and went on in. But not right away.

We approached the entrance with fear and trembling. Maybe it was the sign above the door that said "Danger ahead, enter at your own risk" or maybe it was the total darkness on the other side of that door or maybe it was what Don had said about a guy in Texas who actually went into one of these spook shows and never came out that made me push Don ahead and say, "You go first." Or maybe it was just the gentleman in me.

Whatever the reason, Don was having none of it as he pushed back and retorted, "No, you go first. You're older."

What that had to do with anything was beyond me but it inspired me to come up with my own reason. "Don, you go first. You're younger."

Back and forth we went not realizing that our voices were being projected by the loud speakers over the entire fairgrounds. A crowd had gathered outside the haunted house and seemed to be enjoying our little debate and I think some were even making bets as to who would be first in. Some guy didn't think either one of us would make it. "I bet both of them chicken out."

That was the next to the last straw, the last one being the ticket guy yelling, "You sissies, get on in there."

I figured that I could stay outside and die of embarrassment or go in and die of fright. So I plunged on in. Goodbye, cruel world!

I had moved on into the dark abyss when something hit me on the back of my head. I said, "Don, quit hitting me." I looked around and Don was still standing way back at the entrance.

Suddenly I joined him. Again the ticket man got in on the act saying, "Am I going to have to come up there and lead you by the hand?" Sounded like a good idea to me.

However, for some reason both of us stepped on in ready to risk it all and face whatever it was that lurked inside the spook place - like that slimy something crawling up my back and onto my neck. I yelled and Don screamed. Then Don yelled and I screamed. And we didn't scream for ice cream! It was awful.

"Shall we run?" Don asked. I already was. In just a few seconds I was facing the exit sign. I had made it through – alive and in one piece!

The ticket man looked over at us and said, "Thanks, guys." Seeing our puzzled faces he explained, "Look at this long line. Because of all your screaming and yelling now everybody wants to go through. You guys are the best advertisement for this show we have ever had. And just for that you can go through again. Free."

The gentleman in me replied, "Thanks, but no thanks."

Billy Boy Goes to College

Growing up in Northport means I lived just a hop and a skip from the UA campus. So for this poor boy it was a no-brainer where I would go to college. I sent in my application in August and started in September. I don't think you can do that today but I guess they were desperate for students back then. That would certainly explain why I got in. Either that or they had heard that I was the only football player in the nation who never played a game but whose uniform played almost every down and won All-American honors.

I stayed in Gray's dorm run by my dad and ate most of my meals in Wilma's kitchen run by my mom. Which means that my expenses were almost nothing. I paid thirty-three dollars a month for tuition and a few more bucks for books and except for transportation that was the sum total of my college expenses each semester. I wasn't into fraternities and they wouldn't let me in the sororities so I just concentrated on getting an education. As boring as that sounds.

I hitched a ride with first one and then another. One of those was my future wife who had started to UA earlier and already had parking privileges on campus. Riding with her was a double win for me. I got to get up close to my classes and I got to look at a pretty redhead along the way. I forget if I gave her any gas money but at this late date I'm not going to bring it up because she just might demand back pay and then use that money to go out and buy another dress. She never has anything to wear.

I figure that in my entire college career I probably spent less than a thousand dollars. I'm not rubbing it in to those forking out tens of thousands of bucks today. I'm just thankful I went to college when I did. If I had to pay what they're paying now I could not have gone and would not be the brilliant person I am today.

My parents sent me to college to learn. And I did. I learned not to lock your knees when you're standing at attention in ROTC waiting on the Governor to review the troops. Our flight commander told us that if we kept our knees too rigid (which made it more comfortable to stand for a long period of time) we would cut off circulation in our legs and possibly faint. I thought, "He's got to be kidding. Anybody who can't stand at attention any longer than we're out here has to be a wimp." So said the wimp. I locked my knees, my world turned dark and my stomach turned sick.

"Hey, did you hear about the guy who threw up and fainted in formation yesterday?" That was one of my classmates talking as we strode across the Quad the next day.

All I said was, "What kind of wimps are they sending to this school these days?"

And then I slinked away before somebody could walk up, point at me and proclaim, "Hey, everybody, I've found the wimp!" A person can only take so much humiliation and I was already having enough of that in the classroom.

For one thing, I was struggling to get through Spanish. My professor was a native of Spain and had a way of making even his English sound like Spanish. Of course, it was all Greek to me. But I buckled down and learned how to say, "How are you?" in the language of Spain.

"Como esta usted?"

That's about all the Spanish I can speak today and it makes for some interesting conversations with my Spanish friends.

Here's the English version of one of my conversations in Spanish:
I say, "How are you?'
My Spanish friend replies, "Fine, how are you?"
I respond, "How are you?"
My friend: "You just asked me that."
Me: "How are you?"
Friend: "Are you hard of hearing?"
Me: "How are you?"
Friend: "Are you loco?"
And then I remember another Spanish word I learned so I reply, "Si."

So you see what a great thing a college education is. Not only can I appear dumb but I can do it in more than one language.

IV

School Days, Cool Days

My Love-Hate Relationship with School

SOME PEOPLE HATE ANYTHING and everything about school. They endure twelve years of misery and celebrate the big graduation day with triumphant shouts and great festiveness. I was not one of those people.

Some people just love school. They dream about it at night and spend their weekends looking forward to Monday. Neither was I one of those. My wife was, but not I.

My relationship with school was more love-hate than either one of the above. Here's what I mean.

I loved it when Mr. Hargrove injected his dry humor into his physics lectures. He enjoyed a good joke and had a class full of them. Freddy Glass and Philip Jenkins were two of the biggest. They made the class fun. I hated it when Mr. Dan hovered over me while I was working on a test problem. I do my best work when people are not looking my way. Which is why my grades were nothing to brag about. The teacher kept looking my way. Just think, if only he had looked in the other direction the world could have seen another Einstein.

I hated it when Mrs. Abernathy sent me to the board to diagram a sentence. I was of the conviction that the decent thing to do with sentences is to leave them alone. Let them live in peace. I loved it when Mrs. Irene got off the subject and started telling us her latest hunting adventure. Not that I was into hunting big time, but I was big time into getting away from anything having to do with English grammar.

I loved it when Mrs. Powell patted me on the head and bragged on my reading. That encouragement propelled me into a lifetime of book loving. I hated it when Mrs. Louise called on me to spell hippopotamus. For the sake of all boys and girls in spelling bees they ought to ban that animal.

I hated it when Mrs. Hallman tried to get me to like square dancing. I had two left feet and neither of them worked when it came to swinging your partner around the room. That's why I sent Sharon Evans sailing across the auditorium into the speaker's podium. I loved it when Minnie Ha Ha (a nickname for the teacher I picked up from some of the more unsavory students who shall remain nameless) gathered our class in a circle and read our favorite "Freckles" book. My ideal girl had freckles…and red hair. Twelve years later I married the most beautiful red-headed, freckle-faced woman on the planet.

I loved walking to and from school every day. Especially when I walked past the Patton house and got a glimpse of the beautiful Patton girls. Note: That was the long way around but who cared. I hated sitting in a stuffy classroom for an hour. Even if there was a beauty sitting next to me. Which there usually was because I had great desk selection skills.

I hated it when Mrs. Faucett asked me to stand before the class and give a book report. I thought I would die, but rumor has it that I survived and am still living somewhere in the area. I loved it when she asked me to do things for her because I was the only boy in her study hall. I guess that made me her pet.

I hated it when Mr. Moultrie tried explaining the isosceles triangle to this plane geometry student. The only triangle I was interested in was the one in Bermuda. That class always made me numb on one end and dumb on the other. I loved it when he left the room and John Farrow and I got into a spitball fight. Together John and I were working on a project called "The Various Uses of the Lowly Rubber Band". Okay, Mr. Moultrie didn't buy it either.

I loved walking home from sixth grade with Virginia Henry by my side. The gentleman in me thought she needed an escort and if I was anything at all, it was a gentleman. I hated it when her cousin, Jerry, chased me all over school teasing me about it. I hated the teasing but I appreciated the exercise.

I loved going to the pep rallies in the stadium. Like Hank Williams, all my rowdy friends were there – Douglas Bohannon, George Hunt, Roy Duncan and other assorted felons. I hated spending PE time in the bleachers on Monday picking up trash from last Friday night's game. I was sure I signed up for physical education, not garbage collecting.

I hated it when two boys in Coach Carter's all male home room broke into a fight right next to my desk. I was afraid a wayward punch might come my way. I loved it when Coach made the boys put on gloves and duke it out in the equipment room and invited the whole class to watch – at a nickel a head. With all the yelling and screaming it was as exciting as any match you saw on TV. All that was missing was the root beer.

Then I was very ambivalent about school. Now I mostly love it because if it were not for school I wouldn't have nearly enough to write about in this book.

The All-American in My Family

I was a big star in football. I thrilled my many fans and threatened my opponents by running down the field at lightning speed scoring touchdown after touchdown. More times than I can count I would find myself being hoisted up on the shoulders of my teammates with the head cheerleader hugging the stuffing out of me while planting a big juicy kiss on my cheek exclaiming, "My hero!"

I bet you've already caught on. I bet you've already figured out that all that superstar stuff happened in my mind, not on the field.

But it wasn't for lack of trying.

My chance came in the ninth grade. I weighed a hundred and thirty pounds soaking wet. I know that's hard to believe considering the...ahem...hunk I am today. My mom thought I was too frail to play such a rough sport. She thought I would get hurt. She thought I would never amount to much on the football field. She was right on all three counts. My dad was okay with my football ambition because I think every dad wants his boy to be a star on the gridiron.

I could picture it –

Fan in the stands: Who's that boy running all over the competition and scoring all those touchdowns?

My dad: That would be my son.

Fan: Wow! You must be proud.

Dad: Proud as a peacock in full strut.

So for better or worse I joined the team my freshman year. I was too small, too slow and not very good at all. But I wanted to play in the worst way. Which is exactly what I did. Which is why I'm telling the truth when I say that I was a superlative player. Worst is a superlative.

Our first game was against one of our big rivals, the Holt High Ironmen, out at the old Central Foundry field. Harry Nichols was a star in that game piling up big chunks of yardage as he ran from one end of that field to the other. But old Harry paid a price. Those Holt Ironmen roughed him up and at some point Harry had his jersey torn off his back.

As Harry came trotting to the sideline Coach Dorroh turned to me and yelled, "Gray, take your jersey off and give it to Nichols!" I did. I was a little disappointed that I didn't get into the game but I consoled myself with the fact that my jersey scored several touchdowns that day. I was so proud standing there in my tee shirt watching my jersey sail down the field.

Our next game was in Fayette. Their field was in pretty tough shape – all gravelly and hard as a brick. "I'd hate to hit this ground," I told one of my teamates. Well, I didn't have to worry about that because I didn't get to play. But my shoes did.

In about the second quarter Frank Walker's cleats were coming loose and Coach turned to me and yelled, "Gray, give Walker your shoes!" My shoes made an easy transition from my feet to Frank's and wound up in the end zone a couple of times. You don't know how proud I was of my number tens. Not that I wear a size ten but when you're no good they're not too particular to fit your shoes to your feet. So I came away from the equipment room on uniform distribution day sporting size tens on my size eight hoofs.

Finally, we were back home at the old County High stadium in a rough and tumble game with West Blocton. David Roulaine was playing a super defensive game at linebacker but late in the contest he took a big hit to the head and cracked his helmet. Guess whose helmet went into the game on Roulaine's head? That's right – mine. Three sacks. Wow! Is that helmet good or what!

I never got to play a down that season but my uniform played in every game. I wasn't worth a hoot, but my uniform made All-American that year.

Sixth Grade Prayer Meeting

They say you can't pray in schools any more. But they're wrong. You can pray as much as you want.

Here's my team down five points. If we score on this next play the game will end and we'll be ahead. We will win. So I pray. I bet half the student body is doing the same. Not only am I praying but I'm making promises to God that I'll be a good boy for the rest of the week if only he will let Gene Reynolds or Buster Sullivan or Sonny Wright score this touchdown and move us from the loss column to the win side.

I don't pray for wins anymore and I now get amused at high school and even college and pro players who are earnestly beseeching the Almighty to get on their side. I may be wrong but I don't really think the Good Lord is concerned about who wins a ball game. He has bigger fish to fry. But as long as there are ball games and wins and losses hanging in the balance there will be prayer.

Here's the teacher passing out the test. Here's the student who knows this is going to be tough sledding. So he prays. Personally, I don't know that I ever prayed for an A. Maybe that's why I sometimes wound up on the other end of the grading scale. I always thought that if I didn't buckle down and study I had no right to ask God to ace the test for me.

However, I have to confess that I do pray before tests now. Every Sunday at lunch I ask my grands, three of whom are in UA, "Do you have any tough assignments coming up this week?"

And they tell me, "I've got two tests coming up" or "I've got this paper to write and although I think I'll be okay, it will be a challenge" or "I have a project due on Thursday and I need to do well on it". So I take note and pray throughout the week for these loves of my life. Now you can argue with me all day long about the efficacy of such prayers but I love these kids with all my heart and want to see them succeed in everything they do. So my question is not – should I pray for them to do well, but how could I not pray for them?

I read a book on the meaning of prayer and the author made the statement that if you care for people you will pray for them. Even if you are not necessarily a believer. When your loved one is missing and the hours tick by and still no word, you pray. When your best friend in the whole world is hurting like crazy, you pray. When your favorite couple is on the edge of divorce, you pray. All arguments against the prayer exercise fly out the window. I guess that's why a self-described agnostic like Larry King could write a book on prayer. He feels the urge, too.

I know the feeling. There was one day when the urge hit a whole bunch of us at the same time and we felt that more than private prayer was called for. It was happening at the old Northport Elementary School. I was taking up space in Mrs. Hallman's sixth grade classroom when someone came in with the shocking news that Ray Hamner was involved in a shooting accident and was fighting for his life. We all knew Ray. He was a couple of years ahead of us. Fun guy. Everybody loved Ray. He could put you in stitches with some of the stories he told and some of the things he did.

He was in the class with my cousin, Douglas Holloway, and one day we three were walking down the hall past Miss Ruby Neighbors' room when Ray broke out in a little song about "Ruby-dooby". Cracked us up. Doug got a case of the uncontrollable chuckles and I joined him in the laughing marathon. Such was the effect that Ray could have on you.

And now Ray was wounded. Now he was struggling for his life. Now was the time for all sixth graders to unite and pray for Ray. And pray we did. That group of little boys and girls prayed and prayed that day. Some out loud. Some in silence. But we all prayed. We didn't want Ray to die. We wanted Ray to live. And Ray did live. And now this man is still entertaining his friends and doing good in his community through his service as a fireman and in other ways.

I've thought about that sixth grade prayer meeting a lot over the years. Nobody told us we had to pray. Nobody told us we couldn't pray. We simply felt for a fellow student whom we all liked. So the moment we heard of his plight we prayed. And to this very day I believe with all my heart that we did the right thing.

Pretty Girls Made Me Nervous

When I was a boy I was always nervous around girls. Pretty girls. Let one of these beauties get anywhere near me and I'd break out in a cold sweat and go into stuttering mode when trying to talk.

Senior year. Mr. Hargrove's algebra class. I pick out my desk and plop down. Everything's fine. I'm ready to start a new school year and learn my equations and figure out the meaning of that elusive X. In walks Celia Ann Mims, a very pretty cheerleader, and takes a seat in the desk right next to mine.

Now you may not believe this but something strange happens. Before I have time to get nervous I blurt out, "Hey. I think you are just about the prettiest girl I've ever seen and I'd like a date with you this Friday night."

You're not buying it, are you? I didn't think so. Actually, I get the shakes, my hands get sweaty and my heart starts palpitating like nobody's business. I'm having a meltdown, turning into putty – silly putty at that. I clear my throat and try to speak, but nothing comes out because I have a lump in my throat that takes up half the room. So I give up on the whole venture of striking up a conversation with this beauty and withdraw into my womanless world.

It's not that I didn't want to be around girls, it's just that, as I said, they made me nervous.

Take for example our Blue-White banquet. The Blue-White was our school newspaper and Mrs. Betty Ange, our sponsor, looked over at Nathan Sanders and me and asked, "Who are you guys asking to the banquet?" Is she kidding? She's been with us all semester and doesn't know how inept we are around the fairer sex?

We mutter, "We don't have a date."

She goes into match-making mode, which is a mode characteristic of all women everywhere. "Why not ask one of these pretty girls on the staff?" Now she's got it right that there are pretty girls on the staff. The whole room is filled with gorgeous girls. I think beauty must have been a requirement for admission to this class, which calls for an explanation as to how Nathan and I got in.

"Well, Mrs. Ange, we'll think about it." And I don't know about Nathan but I did think about it. I thought about how the girls would turn me down or how I'd get all nervous even if one of them accepted. I thought about it until I thought myself out of it. And apparently Nathan followed the same thought process because on banquet night there he was without a woman at his side.

So the big moment arrives and I walk into the room at Pete's Steak House and the first person I notice is Jo Ann Haynes, just about the most stunning beauty you've ever laid eyes on. I'm steering clear of this girl who makes Miss America look like a plain Jane. Why, I'd be knocking my tea over and buttering my hand instead of the bread and who knows what else if I were anywhere near her.

So I do the only thing I know to do. I sit next to Nathan. He's not a girl and neither is he pretty. But at least he helps me get through the meal without my making a grand mess.

You're probably wondering how I wound up married to a pretty woman considering my nervous syndrome. So am I.

Boys Will Be Boys when the Class Is All Boys

In this day and time I doubt if you could get away with all the stuff we did in Coach Jimmy Carter's all-boy ninth grade homeroom. Sitting in the corner of the old County High gymnasium we were isolated from the rest of the school – kind of a civilization all to our own. You've heard the old saying, "Boys will be boys". Well, when there are no girls around that is doubly so.

When I was teaching school one of my fellow teachers was always advocating for a segregated teachers' lounge. Not black and white but men and women. He said that men need a place where they can spit and cuss. I'm sure the authorities who figured out the school schedule weren't putting all boys in the same class so we could do the spit and cuss job but I'm glad they separated us. There's just a different dynamic when boys are off to themselves and I'm old-fashioned enough to believe that sometimes this is a healthy thing.

All I can say is that I'm glad that I grew up in a time when boys could be boys and nobody thought ill of it. It was really a lot of fun being a part of that class and I look back on those days as some of my fondest high school memories.

We had some real characters in our class but we were more than matched by the rough and tough and grizzled Coach Carter. When he spoke, we listened. When he barked orders, we obeyed. He had no trouble maintaining law and order with a bunch of rowdy human beings of the male persuasion. Not that some rebel didn't try to get the best of him at times.

One of the boys was caught smoking. I don't remember which one, but the list of possible candidates is quite long. Coach came in telling the felon that he would take a few days to contemplate the appropriate punishment. So after about three days Coach walked in, put a water filled coke bottle on his desk, pulled out a cigarette and dropped it into the bottle. "This is your punishment, boy. When the cigarette is dissolved you're going to drink it down."

Bruce – I mean, whoever it was – protested loudly, "I'm not drinking that stuff!" Coach reminded him that he had not been very particular about what he had put into his body a few days before. So every day all eyes were focused on that coke bottle and every day the culprit loudly protested that he was not going to drink that trashy mess. As far as I know, Coach never did make him drink it. But it certainly weighed on the boy's mind a whole semester.

You can't have a room full of boys without an occasional fight breaking out. Coach wasn't against boys letting off a little steam now and then but he just wanted some order to it. So he carried the fighting next door to the equipment room, put the gloves on the two antagonists and let them slug it out. To the delight of the rest of the class. We were all there gladly paying our nickel to get in and see the big fight. We averaged a revenue producing fight about once a week.

That boxing money was put to good use, funding some charitable cause we wanted to support. Such as Jackie Rushing. This charitable cause was our candidate for ninth grade sweetheart. Since we had no girls in our class the powers that be allowed us our choice of any girl in the entire ninth grade.

Now you have to understand that we had a lot of pretty girls in our school but Jackie was nominated right off. Do I hear a motion that nominations be closed? All of us, being boys and blessed with good eye-sight, were on the Jackie bandwagon. No other nominations were necessary. I mean, the girl was drop dead gorgeous.

Every day for a week Jackie came in during homeroom time trying to raise enough money to win out over the girls nominated by the other classes. She had a fund-raising method that was super successful. She just showed up. Having a face and figure that rivaled Miss America that's all she had to do to empty every pocket of every last cent this roomful of boys had. After all, we hadn't seen a girl in the last twenty minutes. Which translates into an eternity in boy time.

I don't remember if Jackie won or not. But I don't think it mattered to her or to us. She got enough admiring looks for a lifetime and we got enough looking to last until we found our own dream girl.

I Went to the Sock Hops but I Didn't Hop

"Attention all rooms. There will be a sock hop in the gym today during fifth period." Music to my ears. I couldn't wait. Not that I was a dance fanatic. I didn't even know how. But it was a cheap way to get out of class. For a nickel you could miss out on diagramming sentences in Mrs. Darden's English class or fighting another historic battle in Mrs. Williams' history class or embarrassing yourself for not knowing how many senators our state had when Miss Pauline Neighbors called on you in P.O.D. class.

So I never missed a sock hop.

I may not have danced but I liked music about dancing.

"Dance with Me, Henry" was popular in my day. I'd put on that record and when no one was looking stomp all over my room pretending I was Fred Astaire. It was pathetic.

I knew I could never be as good as old Fred but I just wish I could have been as good as Patsy Neighbors when she pantomimed that song at one of our talent shows and blew us all away. You could tell that this friendly to everybody plus size girl was having the time of her life belting out that tune and moving around the stage. And as she danced and sang the whole audience broke out into foot stomping and hand clapping and arm waving and lip whistling.

You go, girl! Everybody really got into it. I always thought Patsy missed her calling – she should have been in show business.

"Let the Little Girl Dance" was another goodie. Here's this guy singing about a "little wallflower on the shelf standing by herself. Now she's got the nerve to take a chance so let the little girl dance." I never got the nerve. But I did go around singing that song a lot. Still do. I know most of the words.

Some of my classmates were really smooth dancers. George Johnson was smooth. So was Carole Glover and Freddy Glass and Beth Moore. A whole bunch of them. I sat in the bleachers watching and admiring and thinking that their feet were made for dancing. My feet – well, they were made for something else. Like walking...or stumbling...or stepping on bugs. Anything but moving in rhythm.

But it wasn't my fault. It was my feet's. I would look down and say, "You guys have really let me down." But they always responded by staying glued to the floor.

When I was a teenager I worked with a man who said that dancing was evil. We boys asked him why? He said that if you take the hugging out of it there would be no dancing. One of the guys spoke up, "What about square dancing? There's no hugging in that."

The man replied, "But it's holding hands." He had us there.

Your sock hop had basically three kinds of people – the dancers, the wanna-be dancers and the wallflowers. I was somewhere between the wallflowers and the wannabes. Some of the dances looked like a whole lot of fun. But to actually dance meant going through the social graces of approaching a girl, asking her if she wants to dance and then actually getting out on the floor in front of a whole roomful of people. So that moved me over from the wanna-be class to the wallflower group.

I guess it was just as well because I met and eventually married a kindred wallflower spirit. We both taught school and chaperoned a lot of proms but never hit the dance floor ourselves. We were excellent observers which is what you want in a chaperone.

So if you visit Margaret and me today and find us in our sock feet it's not because we've been sock hopping. It's just that we are getting ready to rub some liniment on our tootsies.

Study Hall Is for Studying?

The bell rang and I moved toward my seventh period class – a study hall under Mrs. Sarah Faucett. I walked in and sat down and waited for everybody to arrive since I was always early the first day. That was so I could get the seat of my choice which on this day was in the back of the classroom.

One by one the students came in and one by one I noticed these students were different. They wore makeup and dresses and earrings and back then boys wouldn't be caught dead with any of that female stuff. Yep, somehow I had managed to get myself into an all-girl class. And being the sensitive guy that I was, I knew I had to do something. I mean, when the other guys found out about it I'd be doomed to incessant teasing by boys who had nothing better to do than incessantly tease.

So I swung into action. Discovering that there was a study hall of all boys down the hall in Mr. Hargrove's room the same hour of the day I knew what I had to do. I ambled up to Mrs. Faucett's desk and made my pitch. "I think I'm in here by mistake. You see, Mr. Hargrove has all boys in a study hall this period and you have all girls, except for me, of course, so I know there's been a scheduling mistake and I'd like to transfer to the other study hall – the one where the boys are."

One of the front row girls, overhearing me, turned to her friend and said, "Me too!"

Mrs. Faucett smiled and said, "We'd love to have you stay with us, wouldn't we, girls?" They all smiled sweetly. "But I understand" and with that she signed my transfer slip and sent me on my way.

Whew! Glad that was over. I had just saved myself a ton of embarrassment. I couldn't wait to get down the hall to Mr. Hargrove's class and buddy up to all my buddies.

"Mr. Hargrove, here's my slip to transfer to your class. You see, somebody accidentally assigned me to Mrs. Faucett's study hall and since it's filled with all girls I know I'm supposed to be in here."

As I started to hand over my transfer slip some wise guy yelled out loud enough for the whole class to hear, "You mean you're in a class with all girls?"

Uh-oh. I knew it was coming – the embarrassment. But he wasn't done. "You're transferring from a class where you are surrounded by girls to be in here with nobody but boys? Are you crazy?"

And in that moment I had an epiphany. A vision. A moment of clarity. Suddenly the universe made sense.

I grabbed that transfer slip out of Mr. Hargrove's hand before he could change his mind and sped on down to the other end of the building to my all-girl study hall. I may have been slow but I wasn't totally stupid.

I had those girls all to myself until the second semester when George Harbin came in and messed up my little paradise. If you see George, tell him I'm still mad at him.

I Crushed on My Teacher but I Didn't Hurt Her

Did you ever have a crush on your teacher? Beaver Cleaver did. Remember Miss Landers? Opie Taylor did. Remember Miss Crump? So I fell right in with the rich and famous when I had a crush on Mrs. Betty Ange.

It was my senior year and I was getting ready to walk into my Journalism class on the first day of the year. I had always wanted to be on the Blue-White staff and now I had finally made it. Look out, Pulitzer Prize!

I entered the classroom and started surveying the territory. There were so many girls that I thought I had made a mistake and had happened up on a cosmetology class. Then I saw the Nathan boys - Nathan Sanders and John Nathan Wilson and I knew they would never go in for a facial or a nail job. I was in the right place, all right.

So I sat down in the guy section looking over across the room at Mary Carr. I smiled at her because she was such a delightful person. We had been in school together since our elementary days and I had always thought she was one of the sharpest people in our class. She also had a good sense of humor so wanting to have a little fun I tossed a wad of paper her way and called out across the room, "Mary, Mary, quite contrary, how does your garden grow?"

Trying to be cute, I was.

She blurted out behind a deadpan expression, "In the ground, stupid." She then smiled a big smile that meant I got you on that one and I realized that her sharp wit had manifested itself again. And there I sat with no comeback - a witless wonder in Mary's sea of wit.

The bell rang and in walked Mrs. Ange. Wow! This beautiful and shapely lady is supposed to be our teacher? Did I win the lottery or something? Is this payback for all those good deeds I have done (both of them)?

Betty Ange looked young enough to be one of our fellow students. She looked pretty enough to be somebody's girlfriend (actually she was somebody's wife). She looked serious enough to

66

be somebody's teacher. And that's when it happened. This gorgeous creature started orienting us to her expectations for the class and I immediately fell in love. I was smitten. I went all gaga and goofy-eyed. The crush bug had landed on my heart and started chewing. For the next several minutes I was no good to anybody. But then I revived and immediately began working on my strategy.

The rest of the year I did everything I could to get her attention.

I had some experience in getting attention. I remember the night that Linda Ray and I were out on the town together. Linda was our Blue-White editor and a perennial classmate and when I say that we were out together I mean that we both pulled up to the same stoplight at the same time. That should count for something.

There we were at the intersection of Fifteenth Street in front of Stafford Elementary School in Tuscaloosa. I had a carful of crazy guys with me and when Linda pulled up Ronnie Davis looked over her way and exclaimed, "Wow! Look at that gorgeous blonde next to us!"

I looked over at Linda and replied, "Hey, that gorgeous blonde is my classmate." By the way, that gorgeous blonde was at our last class reunion and everybody there agreed that she was the class member who had changed the least. Meaning she's still gorgeous fifty years later.

Switching into show-off mode I told the guys, "Watch this" and then floor-boarding it I scratched off and sent that old '53 Ford flying over the viaduct and down the hill toward Tuscaloosa High. I was chuckling inside thinking how impressed Linda would be with my showy start-off. And no doubt it would have impressed her had it not been for that policeman. The guy on the motorcycle chased me down and pulled me over while the gorgeous gal went zooming by unaware that I was about to be in deep squat. I'm not even sure she ever noticed me.

Sometimes my attention-getting escapades got me nowhere, but sometimes they paid off. Such as in Journalism. I always behaved myself in other classes but in that one I wrote and shared my poems, told jokes, picked on the girls – even nicknamed Barbara Skelton

"Herman". And Mrs. Ange noticed me. She couldn't help but notice me. You may think I'm boasting and I really shouldn't say this, but I became one of her favorites.

I didn't win that Pulitzer, but I did win her attention. And that was enough. I could win the Pulitzer later.

I Was Educated before I Ever Got to School

Fats Domino used to sing about walking to New Orleans. I don't know if I could hoof it that far but I did walk to school every day for twelve years. Now I'm not going to give you any silly nonsense like that fellow who said that he walked ten miles to school uphill both ways in forty below weather. Although, leave out the mileage and the uphill climb and I could duplicate his experience. Well, maybe we could also toss the forty below but it did get cold enough at times to freeze my fanny. And when you have a frozen fanny it inevitably affects the other end. You can't concentrate. Which probably explains why I didn't make straight A's. It was not my head's fault. It was my...well, you know.

But I'm glad I had to walk to school every day. These kids who drive their cars or are chauffeured back and forth don't know what they're missing. Yogi Berra used to say that you can observe a lot just by watching, but I'll amend that to say that you can observe a lot just by walking.

And so I walked. And I observed. And I learned. And here's the story of how I was educated before I ever got to school.

Lesson number one was in the battle of the sexes. It was a Monday – a school day for most of us. But as I passed Fred Ray's house I saw him out washing his car and heard his neighbor, Bill Cadenhead, yelling over to him, "It must be nice to have a holiday from school." To which Fred agreed and kept on washing.

Everybody knew what Bill meant. It was Bear Bryant's second year coaching the Tide and Alabama had just beaten Auburn on Saturday for the first time in a long time and everybody in

Tuscaloosa was feeling so good about it that UA President Frank Rose even declared Monday a holiday for the capstone students.

We've always had our priorities right here in Alabama. Football first, then education. Everybody knows that's the way it's supposed to be.

While Fred was lathering up his vehicle two little boys passed me on their way in the opposite direction to Northport Elementary. I could tell they were in serious discussion about something and when I got close enough to overhear them I discovered what that something was. A girl was on their mind. And not just any girl. This girl was special. I could tell that by the question one of the boys posed to the other. "Can you beat her up?"

To which the other boy replied, "Are you kidding? Tommy says she's the toughest kid in school." Apparently this Tommy fellow had spoken from experience. I can just imagine little Tommy running home with a couple of black eyes and crying, "I don't want to talk about it!"

Well, turn the clock ahead a few years and we all know that these guys will be singing a different tune. Which leads me to a second outside of school lesson – the attraction of the sexes. And I discovered it by walking.

Here I was in the sixth grade and making my daily trek to Northport Elementary when I happened to notice a new girl. This girl was also special – not in the beating up boys way but in the looking good way. I followed her all the way home only to discover that she was a member of the new family who had moved in right across the street from us. What luck!

I developed a strategy. Everybody ought to have a strategy to bring love and happiness to their life. Mine was to make sure that I left for school the same time she did. I mean, it's a free country and I decided if I wanted to walk along with her I could. Well, being kind of on the shy side I actually fell in behind her - but only for a few days until I couldn't stand it any longer and my little heart sent a signal to my dense brain that said, "Do something!"

And I did, finally working up the courage to sidle up beside her and say, "Hi."

She shot a "Hi" back at me and although I should have felt good about her response there was something about the way she said it that was bothersome. It was not a "Hi there, you handsome boy. I'm so glad you're here." It was more of a "Hi, and now that the obligatory greeting is over, get lost."

And I did get lost. But I didn't stay lost. Because of another observation. That girls like to play hard to get. But once a guy is willing to invest in persistence that investment pays off big time. So because of that lesson for the rest of the year I had a girlfriend.

The Day the Sheriff Took Me Away

Nathan Chism was Sheriff of Tuscaloosa County when I was in the sixth grade. The reason I know that is because I remember the day he came to Northport Elementary and took me away in his squad car. Well, it's a long story so let's get started.

I wasn't having a very good day. Oh, it started out all right. I mean, the sun came up in the East and the fresh air was everywhere and Mom had sent me off to school with a hearty helping of bacon and eggs under my belt. Can't beat that for good, can you?

Good day, but bad experiences. I guess it was meant to be. After all, even before I got out of the house there was a bad omen - those holes in my socks that I thought would not matter began to irritate me as my big toes protruded through and were rubbing against my shoes. Annoying as all get out, but I didn't bother to go back inside and change to some unholey socks. I was in too much of a hurry to get to school and tell the guys a joke I had made up during the night. Sixth grade boys live for stuff like this.

Problem number two happened as I approached the old schoolhouse and noticed an old mangy dog lying on school property and I just had to throw rocks at it and chase it away. I chased it right into Miss Christian who at once started scolding me. Have you ever noticed that all teachers are first-class scolders. I think they are required to take Scolding 101 in preparation for teaching.

She gave me a be-kind-to-animals lecture.

"Yes, ma'am. No, I won't ever do that again. I will go right now and give my donation to the Humane Society and volunteer every Saturday for the rest of my life." Well, I didn't say all that, but it was close. From that day forward I'm proud to say that I have never thrown a rock at a dog. Especially when Miss Christian was around.

The next indication that this was not going to be my day was when Mrs. Hallman pulled me aside and scolded me (101, remember) for refusing to help out another teacher when asked to do so. Mrs. Hallman – of all people! She was tough as nails but I had learned that she loved her students and had a heart of gold. I loved her as one of my all-time favorite teachers. And now here she was reprimanding me for being an insensitive cad. This insensitive cad tried to explain that there were extenuating circumstances but I knew she was right. I could do better. And I did do better and wound up a half-way decent human by the end of the year.

And if everything that had happened so far were not enough the Sheriff pulled up. And as he loaded me and three other guys in his car we looked at each other and whispered, "What have we done?"

As we headed off to prison my life flashed before my eyes. Good parents. Good teachers. But then the bad. The time I stole apples from Mrs. Rhodes apple tree. The time Tommy Sullivan and I sneaked into the church sanctuary and fixed the piano so that every time Mrs. Poe hit middle C there was this awful thud sound. The time I mercilessly teased Wanda Parker for spelling my name B-a-l-l-y on a valentine she sent me in the fifth grade. Yes sir, no doubt about it. I deserved a life of incarceration living on nothing but bread and water. I was dirt. I was vermin. I was rotten.

Finally, we arrived at our destination and it wasn't the county jail after all. It was a clothing store in downtown Tuscaloosa. "Boys, since you guys are on the safety patrol we're going to get you fitted for some rubber boots and raincoats to wear on those bad weather days."

I can't tell you how relieved I was. Wait! Yes I can! I was relieved so much so that I didn't even mind the holes in my socks. And other places.

The Night the Stars Came Out

It is 1960. I'm standing in a crowd outside Foster Auditorium on the UA campus trying to get in to see the state championship basketball game between County High and Emma Sansom. Both teams are playing for all the marbles and I want to be there.

It's been quite a ride for our dear old TCHS. Nobody was giving our team much of a chance to win one game in this tournament much less to be in the finals. After all, our Cats posted a mediocre 12-10 in regular season but somewhere along the way the boys in blue gathered enough steam to sail through the first four games of the district tournament before losing to Shades Valley in overtime in the final game. And because this year the top two district teams get to go to the state here is County High ready to show that they are a much better team than their record now reveals.

The most unusual contest of the week has been last night's game with Alexander City. Our guys made a record number of free throws and put it away with a red-hot night at the charity stripe. I was sitting behind the Alex City cheerleaders and one of them complained, "If ya'll weren't making all these free throws we would be ahead."

Well, I couldn't let that charge go unchallenged. "Yeah, well if your guys would quit fouling our guys we'd be making two points at a time instead of one and ya'll would be further behind." Take that!

So she said, "You're mean."

And I said, "You're cute."

She turned her head away as if I had insulted her. But what I'm thinking is that when she got home later that night away from the hostile atmosphere she probably smiled and said to herself, "That handsome County High boy thought I was cute." I'm throwing that handsome part in just to make this story more interesting and because I know my momma would want me to.

Our boys in blue have marched through the tourney bringing down one favorite after another trouncing the highly regarded Coffee of Florence (the complete breakfast team – along with the coffee they could egg you on and serve up the bacon) in the opening round and defeating a solid Albertville team in the semi-finals. And now here we are in the biggest game of all.

I have arrived in what I think will be plenty of time to get a good seat. But some official comes out and says, "Sorry, folks, but we can't allow any more people in because of the fire code."

Hey, what is this! I'm not even going to get in? They can't do this. This is awful. What a disappointment! I cry! I yell! I rave! I pace! I scream! I holler! Not that I'm upset or anything.

Suddenly someone yells from around the corner, "Hey, there's an open window on the second floor and some guy has already scaled the side of the building and gotten in." That's all we need to hear so we run around the corner to check out the situation. A few minutes later I'm sitting down inside the arena ready to watch a great game. No, I didn't break in illegally. For some reason they opened the doors again and we all got in fair and square.

I've never seen so many people at a high school basketball game. It is packed. The whole arena is shaking and quaking. My seat is in the aisle behind the goal but it's high enough that I can see everything. And what I see this night is Clark Boler showing off his hook shot, Buster Sullivan making clutch plays, Harold Bigham and Earl Hydrick playing at their best and Bruce Hutchins putting on a brilliant display of ball control, dribbling that ball like a Harlem Globetrotter. But the guy who steals the show is Duane Brown who hits from the outside all night. I'm talking about from three-point land before there is a three point shot. And every time he misses a basket he gets his own rebound.

I nominate Duane for the all-tournament team. But of course, I have no vote. But if I did he'd be on it.

I go home relishing a state championship – the first and only in school history. And I'm thinking about that girl from Alex City wondering if she really does think I'm handsome.

Schoolhouse Whipping

Did you ever get a whipping at school? For some guys a paddling on the backside is a badge of honor. It's something they talk about the rest of their lives. "Well, kids, your old Grandpa used to get three whippings before lunch period every day." All I can say is that that guy must have had one solid rear end to have held up to that many paddlings a day.

I was inducted into that honor club when I was in the fifth grade. Mrs. Taylor had the privilege of introducing me to our school's butt spanked fraternity. I suppose I was just following in the footsteps of my dad who used to tell us about a whipping he got in the old Mt. Olive Grammar School. From his sister. Who just happened to be his teacher. Aunt Madie whipped him for not paying attention and I can understand that. I only have one picture of my dad when he was a boy but the one I have shows him with this look of devilment as if he's cooking up something he shouldn't do.

It's not often a child has a sister who is his teacher but Aunt Madie was twenty years Dad's senior. He used to tell us kids that one day he would be as old as she was. Of course, we were skeptical, but he proved his point.

"When I was ten, she was thirty which made me one-third her age." Dad was explaining. "When I was twenty, she was forty and I was one-half her age. And when I turned forty, she was sixty moving me to two-thirds her age."

From one-third to two-thirds in thirty years. "You see, it's just a matter of time before I catch up with her." And we kids believed him. Not that we were gullible. We were just good at math.

Back to the badge of honor. My day of induction came one day on the second floor hallway of the old Northport Elementary School. It happened in the lunch line. Harry Nichols tapped me on the shoulder and asked if I had a rubber band on me. Well, of course, I had a rubber band. That was essential equipment in the day of spitball shooting. So I turned my weapon over to Harry knowing he was up to no good.

Whiz, zing! That spitball shot out of Harry's hand and hit Billy Woodard right behind the ear. Harry always was a good shot.

I should have known it but when you're a fifth grader you don't always think of the consequences. I should have known that something like this couldn't be kept quiet. For one thing, Billy was making so much noise you could have heard him all over Alabama. He was in pain. Major pain. He was howling and making all kinds of unjoyful noises. And for another thing, there was a rumbling through the ranks with the eyewitnesses of this commotion saying such things as, "Somebody's gonna get it." They were right.

Remember how Adam blamed Eve for eating the forbidden fruit. And remember how Eve blamed the serpent. That day was the Garden of Eden all over again. We were playing the blame game. Harry was blaming me and I was blaming him and if there had been a serpent around we would have blamed it. However, having no serpent handy I did the only thing I knew to do. I bent over for the inevitable – the paddling. Right there in front of the entire fifth grade. All the rich and famous and everybody. I was too embarrassed to cry aloud. So I just sniffled all the way through lunch period.

Do I need to tell you that I kept that badge of honor secret from my parents? After all, I didn't need another badge.

The Ups and Downs of Life in the Seventh Grade

When you're in the seventh grade in a seven through twelve school, as TCHS was in 1958, you are the low man on the totem pole and at the bottom of the pecking order. And believe me, those upper classmen knew how to peck. I was one of those lowly seventh graders sitting in Mrs. Elmore's classroom trying to listen to her teach us about reading, 'riting and 'rithmetic and yes, sometimes even to the tune of a hickory stick, as the old poem goes. Well, I think she used an oak ruler instead of a hickory stick.

I say I was trying to listen because Douglas Bohannon was vying for my attention whispering his latest joke or calling my attention to a mean looking bug crawling up David Gaut's collar.

Of course, it didn't take much to distract me. After all, I'm kin to my granddaughter, Alex, who after telling me that she'd be glad when her seventh grade was out for the summer I asked, "Don't you like school?" to which she replied, "I like school okay. I just don't like learning."

That's the way I felt in my classroom that day. I guess it's just in our genes. But in our defense I hasten to add that Alex and I both went on to make the Dean's List at UA. I know I'm bragging, but I don't mind it. Especially when it comes to our kiddos.

Life wasn't always easy in and around that classroom out in the annex of old County High. It would have been more serene had it not been for the Hamner boys, Douglas and Donald, terrorizing the junior high playground. But I was okay with their escapades because for the most part I stayed on the good side of these roughnecks.

I think Doug actually liked me ever since that day when Mrs. Elmore was calling the roll asking for each student to give his or her full address. Everybody was telling house and street and avenue numbers and I guess I wasn't paying much attention because when it came to my turn and she asked, "Billy, where do you live?" I blurted out, "Over behind Holman Lumber Company right at the foot of Mitchell hill."

The whole class exploded with laughter and I thought Douglas was going to fall out of his desk. Ever thereafter, he looked on me kindly. Maybe it was just his feeling sorry for an ignoramus.

However, there was this one time when we almost tied up out at the playground. For some reason I was mad at Douglas and itching to pick a fight with him. Now that sounds strange to somebody who knows me – knows that I wouldn't hurt a flea - but here I was ready to inflict some major pain on my fellow student.

You know how it is when you're looking for an opportunity to do something that you shouldn't do – you'll always find it. And one day I found mine. Right there in the middle of a football game on the junior high playground. I caught a pass and started making that sustained groaning sound that I had heard Bill Tucker make at varsity football practice. I thought I was big time. Douglas laughed and yelled out, "Listen at old Gray acting like one of the big players!"

Normally I would have laughed along with Douglas. But remember, I was looking for a fight. So I threw that ball to the ground and ran over and got right in Doug's face. "You wanna make something of it?"

Doug, whose smile was now missing, bumped up against me and countered, "Yeah, I do!" Bumping and staring we were each ready for the kill until Doug finally laughed again and said, "Let's play ball."

I know why he did that. He got to thinking of my address over behind Holman Lumber Company at the foot of Mitchell hill and couldn't contain his laughter. And you can't fight a guy while rolling on the ground. I'm really glad that it happened that way because when I got home I realized that if it had come to fists Douglas would have mopped up that playground using my body as the mop. And even though I'm not Catholic somebody would have said the last rites over me and I would have never set foot in that old schoolhouse again. I would have remained in a purgatory of ignorance.

That was the year of two significant races that happened right there on the seventh grade playground. I'm sorry that you can no longer see the mark where it all took place because they obliterated it when they built the new Adrian McKinzey Gymnasium. Just take my word for it, it was there.

The first race happened the day Roy Duncan walked over to me and said, "I can outrun you." All the guys were talking about how fast I could run and apparently Roy had had enough of such talk so he was challenging me.

I laughed and waited for the punch line - the very idea of somebody as big and slow as Roy thinking he could even stay in a race with the track king of Fourteenth Street. But there was no punch line and Roy proceeded to run my pants off. Not a good feeling to be pantless in the middle of the playground.

The second race found me outrunning one of the fastest guys in the school. I'm talking about Wade Booth. Now you probably think I'm lying. You're thinking that I could never outrun one of the fastest guys in the school, probably the speediest back on our football team.

That just shows what you know. You don't know how fast a fellow can run when his life is threatened.

When Wade told me to get off the playground I said no. I mean I had as much right to be there as anybody. And then he ran at me and I said bye. So I hot-footed it out of his way in world record time so that he and his brother Douglas could have all that space to themselves. You can do some pretty amazing stuff when you're running for your life and I was determined that I was not going to spend the rest of my life dead.

I now believe that I should have stood up to Wade. I just know that I could have gotten the better of him that day. Here's how it would have happened: Before he took that first swing I would have reminded him that my address was over behind Holman Lumber Company at the foot of Mitchell hill. That would have done it. He would have lost it. He would have hit the ground rolling. He would have become putty in my hands.

Thanks, Wade, for not jumping on me and making me bring you down that way. It would have been embarrassing for both of us.

The Pitch

I was on the pitcher's mound getting ready to bedazzle my opponents. Why my team chose me for such an important job was anybody's guess. Guess number one: It was my softball. Wrong. It was the school's softball. Guess number two: I was famous for striking out all comers. Wrong. I was not famous nor did I strike out anybody (the one exception I'll explain in a moment). Guess number three: I beat everybody to the mound. Right. I may not have been much of a pitcher but I was a champ at beating everybody to the mound.

We were a bunch of seventh graders playing our game on the playground next to the gym. We shared the area with a lot of people including some senior high girls in Treva Smith's PE class. My sister was one of those girls and when I saw her out of the corner of my eye I thought I'd show her and all her friends of the fairer sex just how good her little brother was. No doubt they would quit hanging around football stars like Gene Reynolds and the Brown boys – Johnny Mack and Leon - and start noticing me. After the display of talent I was about to unleash the whole world would be paying attention to me and my new pitch. There was no doubt about that in my fantasy riddled mind.

So I wound up and threw my Billy Boy slowpoke special. It was a pitch I had seen Rex Oliver deliver in church league softball. Rex threw that ball so slow that you could have quoted the entire Gettysburg Address while it was in flight to the batter's box. I was amazed at the number of people who struck out trying their best to hit that slow moving ball.

I couldn't wait to try it out. And now the opportunity presented itself at just the right time. I kicked my feet into the old dirt mound, spit a couple of times, tugged on my britches and adjusted my cap.

I was ready. I wound it up and delivered my Billy Boy slowpoke special. "Fourscore and seven years ago our fathers…" Well, you get the idea. It took that ball forever to get from my hand to the plate and when it finally arrived the guy swung for the fences but only got thin air. Whiff! Strike one! I did it two more times all the time looking to see if my sis was watching. She was.

She had witnessed my strikeout but at the supper table that night all she said was, "You pitch like a girl." What! Melna Gayle Gray, my sister, my own flesh and blood saw the pitch of a lifetime and all she can say is that I pitched like a girl! Of course, I have to admit, the slow pitch did look kind of sissy.

She continued, "Daddy, you've never seen a ball go that slow." Then looking at me she added, "You better eat some more cornbread and peas, boy." And glancing over toward Mom she nodded, "Mama, pass Billy an extra helping of that stuff." Big sister was on a crusade to make the weak strong.

That's just like a sister. Notice the slow ball and ignore the strikeout. Notice the weak pitch and ignore my brilliant strategy. Of course, I was ignoring some stuff of my own. Like noticing the strikeout but ignoring what the next batter, Larry Bonner, did slamming that ball all the way to next Thursday (and this was on a Tuesday). And so did the next and the next and… Well, there's no reason to go on and on with this nonsense.

That's the reason I no longer deliver the Billy Boy slowpoke special. That and the fact that this macho guy doesn't want anybody thinking that he throws like a girl. Unless that girl is my little sister who can outplay most boys. Or that girl is any girl who is on a fast pitch softball team. Or that girl is any girl who doesn't have her arm in a sling.

Slap Happy

I remember the day the prettiest girl in school slapped my face. That was Jackie Rushing. Okay, if you were in Northport

Elementary at the time and want to argue about it I'm sure you could come up with other candidates that could hold that title. Celia Ann Mims, Rosemary Palmer, Polly Lindsey, Olivia Lake, Wanda Parker...should I go on? All of them could turn your head. I know they turned mine. But I have to go with Jackie because if I don't I won't have a story. None of these other girls slapped my face. They may have wanted to, but they didn't. Only gorgeous Jackie had that distinction.

Jackie and these other girls were not just good-looking. They were good at everything they did. Such as square dancing. They were always in group one – the best dancers. I'm talking about Hall of Fame talent. I was in group five – the worst dancers. I'm talking about Hall of Shame talent. So most of my square dancing time found me standing with the rest of the rejects looking over at the kids who knew how to really shuffle those feet. I admired them.

But that wasn't for me. For some reason I just couldn't get into swinging your partner round and round. When the caller yelled, "Promenade" I grabbed my girl and just about flung her all the way out the door. And when the call came for us to do-si-do – well, what in the world is a do-si-do? By the time I figured it out all the other boys and girls were working on another dance move. The pas de deux. Wait! That's a ballet move. But you get the idea.

So I drug my feet through the whole hour. I hated the class so much that between the classroom and the square dance pad outside I got lost. Intentionally. I had found an out of the way spot and spent do-si-do time in my hideout. I really thought I would get into deep trouble until I discovered that for some reason Mrs. Hallman didn't miss me. Maybe she was grateful that she didn't have to worry about that boy who has four eyes and two left feet. I don't know.

It was not only in square dancing class that we were divided into groups, but also in everyday school life. I could identify at least three major ones. I call them the "haves", the "have-nots" and the "have-whats". The "haves" were the kids who lived on the right side of the tracks. You know, the brightest and richest and best connected. They were usually the best square dancers, too. The "have-nots" were the kids from the wrong side of the tracks. They wore hand-me-downs and had holes in their socks. The "have-whats" were the kids in the middle – not having everything but still not having nothing either.

I had friends in all three groups. I identified with the "have-nots" because I sometimes had holes in my underwear (although my mom would whip me for saying that because she always insisted on clean and untattered fruit of the looms– you know, in case you had a wreck). I identified with the "haves" because in fifth grade I had the smarts to put down everybody in a spelling bee (I know I'm bragging, but I don't mind). And I lived most of my life in the average middle of the "have-whats" world (I was middle material before Malcolm ever showed up). But I liked them all. I figured that if you're going to have to spend the major part of your growing up years with all these people you might as well try to get along.

Well, back to the slapping episode. Recess was almost over and a group of us gathered in a circle in Mrs. Hallman's sixth-grade class telling jokes and funny stories when somebody told a joke about Jackie. And everybody laughed. I mean, everybody. I don't think Jackie liked it very much because she frowned up and walked over and planted one on my face – and I don't mean a kiss. Slap! Take that!

I could have protested, "Hey, why hit me? I mean everybody laughed?" But I didn't protest. I could have cried and silently slipped away to some corner and brooded. But I didn't do that either. I mean the prettiest girl in school just slapped my face and I wasn't upset in the least. I was just glad she was paying attention to me.

V

The Old Neighborhood

I Played in Yankee Stadium

HERE'S A LITTLE KNOWN fact, one that I certainly don't mean to brag about – I played in Yankee Stadium. Here's another well-kept secret - Yankee Stadium is located right here in Northport. I bet those two statements surprise you. I bet you're thinking, "That Gray kid never was good enough to play on his high school team much less in Yankee Stadium. And besides, I know where Yankee Stadium is – it's in New York."

You know what your problem is? You just can't think like a teenage boy who has a vivid imagination.

I was just a kid who lived on Fourteenth Street. And as far as I and a dozen other boys were concerned we played in the best arena ever. It was right across from my house. Okay, everybody else just saw a vacant lot but we neighborhood guys saw Yankee Stadium. They say that beauty is in the eye of the beholder. Well, so is a stadium.

We had all the things the more famous stadium had.

Bleachers. We could seat everybody who wanted to watch us play on the steps attached to the back porch of the house across the bushes behind home plate. There was a gap in those hedges which made it possible from that vantage point to see everything you needed to see.

Here's the runner coming home from third and tagged just as he's crossing the plate. Is he out? Is he safe? We start arguing about it and some of the fans even run out on the field and yell, "He's safe!" matched by others yelling just as loudly, "He's out!" And after much dickering someone exclaims, "Play ball!" and we go back to hitting and catching and all those things little boys love to do with a baseball. And the fans return to the stands until another close call sends them flying back out to the field to put in their two cents worth. What other stadium allows their fans active participation in the game? Not even the real Yankee Stadium has that.

VIP section. That was Mom and Dad sitting on our screened-in front porch across the street. On a clear day when the nearby sawmill wasn't covering the area with a cloud of smoke they could see all the way to center field although they would have a little trouble identifying the player who was covered by grass and bushes and vines and whatever else lurked out there in the outfield of our famous stadium. And on those days when my Uncle Virlin and Aunt Ann came over for a visit the VIP box doubled in attendance.

Concessions. Mr. Junior Davis' quick-stop store was just down the street around the curve and up the hill. In between innings we would take time out for a coke and some chips – fans, players and everybody. For a quarter you could buy all the snacks you wanted. What a sweet deal!

Parking lots. Every driveway at every house surrounding our field was available for our fan base. While most of our admirers walked to the stadium, every now and then someone would drive up in a '56 Ford, pull into one of the driveways, race his engine and just sit there until the inning was over and we all had a chance to ooh and aah over this marvelous machine that you could hear six blocks before it ever arrived. After a few minutes going over the machine it was "play ball" time again and we were back to business. How many major league fields do you know that have a car show right in the middle of the third inning?

Even though our place could match the more famous stadium and was even superior in some ways I have to admit the New York stadium had something we didn't. Smooth and well-groomed grounds. The best you could say about our field is that it was uneven with washed out ditches so huge they could qualify as gullies. Hit a fly ball to the infield and the second baseman would yell, "I got it!" and then suddenly disappear into one of those ravines before re-emerging on the other side of the big ditch in time to make his play on the runner who had left first base.

And if you had outfield duty you had to stand across the street in the high grass next to the woods beside Sandra Hunter's house where you not only could lose baseballs but baseball players in that thick brush. We had one guy who went missing for five innings. Well, that's an exaggeration – it was only four innings.

Our field, washed out and barren in some places and filled with every variety of grass and plant in other places, was a challenge to even the best players. A good hitter knew how to hit the ball just enough to go over second base and land on the pavement of the street that ran several blocks downhill. And a good fielder was one who could run out of the knee high grass into the street and chase and retrieve the ball before it rolled all the way into downtown. Needless to say you had to be in tip-top shape to play this game on our field.

All in all it was quite an experience. I'm just glad I had the opportunity to play in Yankee Stadium.

The Game of the Century

I was there at the game of the century. No, it was not Super Bowl III when Joe Namath led the New York Jets to a 16-7 win over the highly favored Baltimore Colts. Namath had promised a victory for his team and had made good on his promise. Who could ever forget that?

I was there at the game of the century. No, it was not Bama's big Sugar Bowl win over Miami in the January 1, 1993 game that secured a perfect season and the national championship for the Tide when all the experts were saying that Miami would win big. Who could forget the Bama blow-out with the Tide breathing down the neck of the Hurricane's All-American Heisman winning quarterback all night?

I was there for the game of the century. But it wasn't the college all-stars' surprising 20-17 victory over the NFL champion Green Bay Packers. I knew the college guys were going to win it when early in the game Lee Roy Jordan, Bama's All-American linebacker, stopped the Packers All-Pro fullback Jim Taylor dead in his tracks. The mighty Packers were being humbled by old Lee Roy and company.

Maybe other games come to mind as to the game of the century. But the one that stands out to me and I think certainly qualifies for the game of all time was one hardly noticed by anybody. But I noticed. As a matter of fact, I was a participant in that game to end all games.

It took place in my back yard.

Bill Tucker lived across the street from me and every once in awhile he'd saunter on over for a game of one on one basketball. We'd start by announcing who we were. Today Bill is Ohio State and I'm Michigan. Another day he is Kentucky and I am UCLA. Maybe next time he will be Indiana and I'll be Ole Miss. Since both of us were Tide fans we ruled out either of us being Alabama.

So on the day of the famous game we stood under the basket and named our team.

Bill: "I'm Ohio State."

Me: "I'm Keyoak."

Bill did a double take. "Say what?"

I explained, "It's a team I made up."

And I had made it up - created this whole football world in my boyish mind with Keyoak, a super good team, at the top of the heap. In my fantasy Keyoak never lost a game in any sport. Year after year they went undefeated.

How good was Keyoak? Well, they were so good that sometimes their QB would fade back for a pass but before chunking the pigskin downfield he'd pull a ukulele out of his uniform and serenade the fans while the line held off the rush. Of course, after the last bars of the melody he'd throw a perfect spiral to the open receiver in the end zone. And the crowd would go wild.

I loved that play. Loved that ukelele. Such was the strength of Keyoak.

So this day when I named Keyoak as my team I was putting everything on the line. Their undefeated record, their reputation, their uke concert in the backfield – everything.

I was taking a huge risk because Bill almost always beat me in these games. He was thirteen and I was ten. He was taller and stronger and better all around. He would later make All-County. But that was in football and this was basketball. Besides, I had the edge in motivation. I was defending a record no other team in the world had come close to achieving. I had to win this game. Just had to.

Bill and I squared off – Ohio State and Keyoak. Bill scored. I scored. Bill missed and I got the rebound. I missed and Bill got the rebound. Who would be first to get to twenty? Who would be the winner? I was ferocious. I was mean. I was tough. I was like an attack dog. I was relentless. I was all over Bill on every play. I hustled for the rebound. I went after the ball every time Bill got his hands on it.

After several minutes and a lot of huffing and puffing the score was tied at eighteen apiece. Bill had the ball. I was nervous – sweating – heart throbbing ninety to nothing. Bill drove toward the basket and put the ball up. It went round and round the rim and then careened off to the side. I fought furiously for the rebound – fought harder than I had ever fought for anything in my life. And it paid off.

Suddenly the ball was in my hands and I knew what I had to do. I moved toward the basket and then out again. Back to the basket and out once more. I was keeping Bill guessing. I faked left and went right and suddenly seeing an opening I drove to the basket once more – this time putting that ball up in a do or die layup. It hung in mid-air for what seemed like an eternity. And then finally – swish! The sound I wanted to hear.

It was over! I had won! I had won! I had won! Keyoak remained undefeated never to lose a game to this very day.

So what did I do to celebrate? I pulled out a ukulele and sang a song. Which, by the way, was the song of the century.

Cow Pasture Football

We guys were sitting around one day chewing the fat and trying to figure out our next adventure. At the time there were about a dozen boys living in our neighborhood and a dozen more down the street near the old Northport train depot. I'm talking about guys like A. L. and Larry Wilson and James and Bill Swartz.

Our block had a James, too. James Eads was our leader and this day he had an idea that he thought would be a lot of fun and since fun was our middle name we listened to his pitch. "I was talking with some guys out in Coker the other day and they want to get up a football game with us and play in somebody's cow pasture out there."

Thus I was about to be introduced to cow pasture football. It's a brand of football with its own unique rules which are basically that there are no rules. But there are some understandings.

One, you understand that if you show up you play. That day in Coker about forty boys showed up and all forty played. The whole game. No substitutions. We figured that any guy who was there was chomping at the bit to get some playing time so no matter how many were already on the field and no matter how good or bad the guy was he got his chance.

What you were shooting for was to have more good players than bad ones on your side, but they were all mixed in with everybody included and it was a whole lot of fun. None of this – he can't play because he's not good enough. Okay, if he's no good then just don't throw him the ball. Unless, of course, he winds up in the clear in the end zone. The sorry players tended to go unnoticed and would find themselves free and clear every now and then. I know – I found myself free and clear every now and then.

Another understanding – you take yourself out of the game whenever you need a break and you put yourself back in after you catch your breath. You'd think that with all that blood and sweat and tackling and blocking that a kid would want to sit out for awhile. Not so. There's something about teenage boys that makes them want to hang in there to the bitter end. The rougher the better.

One more understanding – each guy calls the penalties as he sees them. Here's the way it worked for us: if you went out for a pass and the defender was holding you, you yelled to high heaven, "Hey, interference!"

And of course, the accused would yell, "I didn't touch him!"

So then we argued it out until we came to a mutual agreement as to what actually happened. You'd think that wouldn't work. But it did. You'd think our discussion would take up too much time and slow the flow of the game. But it didn't. It's amazing what boys can accomplish if they're left alone. I've seen more games ruined by adults interfering than by any kid.

In cow pasture football we learned a lot about life – give and take, calling'em as you see'em, making your case, the necessity of negotiation. Stuff like that. And of course, using the cow pasture as our field, we also learned a lot about watching your step. If the opposing player didn't get you the cow pad might. So, as Andy Griffith once said, the object of the game is to see who can take that funny looking pumpkin and run from one end of that cow pasture to the other without either getting knocked down or stepping in something.

And I might add, if you stepped in something, you walked home...alone.

I Used to be Tall

I was the shortest kid in the fourth grade. Okay, maybe I had that distinction in the first, second and third grades, too, but it didn't dawn on me until one day in Mrs. Louise Powell's fourth grade class when she sorted us students according to height. We were lining up to go to lunch and maybe she felt sorry for us little fellows or maybe she thought we ought to get a head start on eating or maybe she just thought we were the cutest (my favorite option) so she put us at the front of the line.

She couldn't quite figure out who was the shortest among three of us – Bobby Hamner, Joseph White or me – so she alternated who would actually lead the gang down to the lunchroom. That meant I got to be first every third day. Bobby eventually became tall but Joseph and I stubbornly held true to our shortness. Until one day... Well, I'm getting ahead of myself.

I often wondered what it would be like to be tall, to look down on everybody instead of always looking up. I read an interview with James Arness who played Marshall Matt Dillon on Gunsmoke. He said that in his pre-Gunsmoke days he spent most of his time on the movie set digging holes to stand in so that his 6'7" frame wouldn't tower over the leading man.

Now, there's an idea. What if I got all the tall people to stand in a hole whenever they were around me? That means I could have looked at Polly Lindsey eye to eye instead of eye to chin. Later when I actually grew to be almost at eye level with Polly I discovered that her whole face was pretty, not just her neck. I had been missing a lot.

You can see my dilemma – how to make a short person tall. Of course, I knew that tall people digging holes to stand in wouldn't work. What about those times when we'd be standing on concrete? And what if one of the tall ones refused to dig? You have to think these things out carefully.

No, I'd have to look for another solution. And then one day I found it.

I looked out my window one morning and saw Earl Mitchell coming down the hill from his house towering over the hedges that lined the roadway – the hedges that obscured part of the road from my vantage point. I knew Earl was tall but this morning he looked unusually so. When he finally came out into the clear I could see what was going on – he was walking on stilts. Tom walkers as we called them. They projected him up into the air about three or four feet beyond his usual height.

"Hey, Billy, want to be tall?" Hey, I've lived for this moment! So we got busy and made me a pair of those stilts. And for the rest of the day Earl and I walked around the neighborhood looking down on everything and everybody. We even had a stilt race around the house. Of course, I came up short. But at least I was tall when I was short. Which was still a good feeling.

But alas, I eventually put the Tom walkers away realizing they were no permanent solution. How would I ever get those leggy things over my pants? No, I'd just have to resign myself to being short. And I did. And I have. Which is not bad. Not bad at all.

Actually, there are certain advantages to being closer to the ground. For instance, you can more easily spot the loose change people have dropped. Why, if I had been tall all these years I wouldn't have seen all those pennies lying there for the taking and that would have left me about...oh... forty-seven cents poorer. That's a lot to give up just to be tall.

And I also discovered that the good Lord knew what he was doing when he made me short. I'm afraid of heights. So if I were as tall as someone like my friend Brian Harvey, who reaches into the stratosphere, I'd be drunk dizzy all the time.

So I've learned to be content to have my legs just long enough to touch the ground. I wouldn't have it any other way.

Tarzan and the Poor Boys

A group of us boys got together one day and somebody mentioned that a great double feature Tarzan movie was playing at the Ritz Theater. Well, we just had to go – I mean, double the Tarzan – you just don't ignore something like that.

We pooled our money to see if we had enough for all of us to get in. We did. Barely. We would have to be content to just smell the popcorn and quench our thirst at the water fountain.

The Ritz was located in downtown Tuscaloosa and here we were in Northport two miles away. But we never gave it a second thought as to how we would get there. Walking was our mode of transportation. That was a given since we belonged to one car families and our dads drove that one car to work. So if we didn't want to be stuck at home we hit the pavement. Frankly, the good times were mostly in the going and coming more so than in the destination.

Walking through downtown Northport and crossing the river bridge, we finally arrived at the Ritz ready to take in one of our all-time favorite super heroes. We looked forward to admiring Tarzan's muscles and whistling at the beautiful Jane and laughing at the funny antics of Cheetah.

I walked up to the ticket booth and plopped down just enough money for three adults and one child. Three of us boys were teenagers and of course, had to pay the adult fare while Don could get in on a child's ticket since he was only eleven. Or so I thought. Imagine my surprise when the lady asked our ages and Don blurted out, "I'm twelve." That meant full price. That meant no Tarzan because that meant we had insufficient funds.

I interrupted, "No, Don, remember you're only eleven." Don objected saying that he had turned twelve just last week. I was honest in my belief that he was eleven, but that was the last honest thing I did all day. I hit Don on the shoulder and asked the lady to excuse us as I escorted the former eleven year old around the corner for a serious conversation.

"Don, here's the situation. We have just enough money if you are eleven so you're going to tell that lady that you are not twelve."

Don suddenly turns Mr. Pious. "Won't that be lying?"

"Well, of course, but it's just a little one."

He kept on, "I'm not supposed to lie." This is the kid who told his parents that he was going to school and then hid out in the woods all day playing hooky. For a whole week!

I eyed Don with this look of desperation and asked, "Do you want to see this movie or not?" He said he did. "Then you're eleven." And back to the ticket booth we went.

"I'm sorry, Miss, but the boy was just a little confused. He's actually eleven." She didn't buy it since the cat was already out of the bag, so to speak. After a season of begging and pleading the ticket selling lady asked us to leave. Which we did. But we didn't go too far because as luck would have it, somewhere between the theater and the corner drug store we happened up on a shiny quarter lying on the sidewalk.

Around to the ticket booth again. We were smiling big time anticipating finally getting in to see these great jungle movies. The ticket woman counted out the money I had plopped down. I could just hear those African drums and that famous Tarzan yell reverberating through the jungle.

But it was not meant to be. Shaking her head she said, "You're still short."

What! How could that be? Well, it seems that while Don and I were having our age discussion Odis had gone into the drug store and bought a sucker with some of the show money leaving us a lollipop's worth short of the necessary funds.

About that time my friend Mickey came out of the movie raving about how these were the best Tarzan movies ever. I turned to Don once more. "Are you sure you're not eleven?"

The Longest Arms in the World

He's not listed in the Guinness Book of World Records, but in my estimation he should be. I'm talking about Billy Woodard, my high school friend and boxing companion. I never expected mild mannered Billy to turn into Superman in the ring. But that's what he did one day at my expense.

My cousin, Douglas Holloway, bought some boxing gloves and then recruited every boy in the neighborhood to enter a boxing tournament over at his place. I dropped by his house the day the gloves arrived and learned that Doug had already put our uncle, Jerry Smelley, on the canvas. Jerry was only a few years older than us so Doug coaxed him to put on the gloves and get in the ring for a little demonstration.

Little demonstration, big hit. One swing and Jerry was on the canvas. Well, it wasn't actually canvas – it was the hard ground. And it wasn't exactly a ring either – it was the great outdoors of Doug's back yard.

Now you need to know that cousin Doug was about 230 pounds strong while Uncle Jerry was considerably less. I don't know if Jerry just wasn't paying attention or simply underestimated Doug's famous right but the next thing he knew there was this gloved fist hitting him square in the face and it was floor time for Jerry. But the uncle didn't say uncle because just as soon as he hit the ground he was back up ready to give Doug what for.

I don't know if Doug was afraid that he might get whipped or that he might hurt his uncle but he immediately pulled off the gloves and said, "I'm through." But in spite of that temporary respite from the sport this was the beginning of a lot of boxing activity on Holloway Hill.

The boxing commissioner – that would be Doug - paired us boys according to size and age and put us in the ring to see how we'd do with the gloves. In comes Billy Woodard, my opponent. Our ring was a rope laid on the ground in a square so if you were on the ropes that meant you were on the ground. Which is where I was after a few minutes into the first round...or was it the second? I don't remember. What I do remember is saying to myself, "I can take this guy."

Famous last words. This is where the world record comes in. Billy had to have the longest arms in the world. How else can you explain his fist reaching my face a dozen times before I could land a decent punch? Not only were his arms longer than anyone else's, but he had more than the usual two. Boxing gloves came at me from every direction. I thought I was fighting an octopus.

After round one I came to my corner and said to my manager – which also was Doug – "I never knew Billy's arms were that long. Did you know that his arms were that long?"

Doug kept rubbing my gloves and encouraging me. "You just gotta hang in there. Wear him down." I looked at Doug like I didn't know the meaning of what he was saying.

The bell rang and I was back out there for more of the same. Billy hit me five times before I could blink my eyes. I was thinking not only has this guy got long arms but they're on some kind of super-charge. Nobody can swing that fast.

I came back to the corner. My beloved corner. It looked so good. Can I stay here forever? Doug told me that I need to up my tempo. Hit him before he hits me. So armed with a new resolve and good information I bolted out of my corner determined that I was going to get in the first punch. I swung really hard and fast and somehow hit my own face. Then Billy swung and hit my own face.

What has everybody got against my face?

Finally, the bell sounded again and it was over. Billy won by a decision. I decided not to get back into the ring.

That wasn't the first or last time I got a whipping, but it was the only time I got whipped wearing boxing gloves.

I never put on the gloves again. I decided to hang it up before something serious happened – like having my nose transferred to the side of my face instead of the customary middle. I retired from my boxing career early so we'll never know how great I could have become if I had stayed with it. But I didn't stay with it. I figured that putting an end to getting beat up was the least I could do for my mom. She never liked seeing her only son get hurt. And her only son never was too fond of the idea either.

Basketball Goals I Have Known

In the almost words of Will Rogers, I've never met a basketball goal I didn't like. And I've met quite a few. Maybe as many as the boys in Fayette. That's the town in our neighboring county and just up the road from us. Back in the fifties and sixties their school had some of the best basketball teams in the state and I always wondered how they managed to be at the top year after year. I found out one day as I drove through Fayette County and saw a basketball goal in every yard in the whole county. They live and breathe basketball up there.

And that's the way we were. Some of us. I'm talking about the boys I grew up with. You could always find a goal surrounded by a bunch of basketball loving kids. Consequently, I got acquainted with a lot of basketball goals during those years.

When you think of a basketball goal in a yard you usually picture a lone long post driven into the ground with a goal attached. Not so with Ronnie Davis' goal. He had the best basketball facility I've ever seen in someone's yard. I guess his dad knew we neighborhood boys were going to be playing a lot of basketball and maybe he figured that one day one of us would become famous at the sport (we were awesome looking) so he fixed up a first class court.

It had nice sturdy goals with new nets and a concrete floor that you could actually bounce a ball on without it careening off to one side. There were even bleachers of a sort. Concrete walls were positioned on three sides of the court and the top made for a nice seat where our many fans sat – Ronnie's sister, Donna Fay, and the local cat whose name I can't recall at the present time.

Now Earnest Porter's goal was a different matter. Rickety and rusty and leaning to one side this goal on the south end of his yard still attracted guys from miles around. The Bridges brothers, O'Neal and Alton, Tommy Dockery, Bill Tucker, Billy Hall, Pot Miles (yes, you read that right – his real name was Charles but in the South we like our nicknames – the pottier the better), Earl Mitchell, Dale and Leroy McKinley, Frank Kemp and of course, Earnest. And me. These were just a few of the guys who showed up at Porter Court. Sometimes we had as many as fifteen to twenty boys all playing at the same time (we didn't believe in substitution). Sometimes it was more like "Last Man Standing" than it was basketball. But it was great fun.

Earnest's goal had no net. We'd put the ball through the hoop and then get ready to chase that rascal down the hill before it got to the creek that ran through the pasture behind the Porter homestead. And the back yard slanted downward so you not only had to keep an eye on your opponent but on the ground, too. Alternating between hilly and holey that unlevel terrain could send that ball sailing southward any time you bounced it. If it hadn't been for our great dribbling skills we would have had to call timeout every few minutes just to chase the ball.

The most unusual goal of all was not even a goal. My dad took a vow of poverty when it came to buying me a basketball goal so I had to make do. And an old chinaberry tree in our yard was my do. The trunk jutted up about ten feet before splitting in two directions and right in the middle of that split was a flat place that would have been a perfect spot for a goal. So I visualized one being there. I'd spend hours shooting at that make-believe goal and it wouldn't be long until all the neighborhood guys would join me around that old chinaberry. And all any passers-by could see were these crazy kids bouncing a ball against a tree. If only they could have seen what we saw.

Another basketball goal was inside my house. Some people have an indoor swimming pool. I had an indoor basketball court. Well, actually it was my bedroom which I turned into a gymnasium. I took the globe off the light, turned it upside down on the bed and shot at it with wads of paper. Of course, dribbling was out of the question, but I solved that problem. I imagined myself dribbling. If you can imagine a wadded piece of paper as a ball you can imagine dribbling a piece of wadded up paper.

Over the years I've seen a lot of super nice basketball goals in some super nice arenas. But I wouldn't trade any of them for playing with a bunch of amateurs in Davis Gym, Porter Court or Chinaberry Tree Square Garden.

My Blue 20-inch Girl's Bike

I had just moved into the neighborhood and was eager to get acclimated to my new setting when I spotted some boys riding their bikes up and down the street. That's all I needed so I jumped on my little blue 20-inch girl's bike and peddled toward this gang of guys. As I pulled up somebody yelled out, "Hey look, guys, this kid is riding a girl's bike. A 20-inch girl's bike at that." They all laughed and began to make fun.

It didn't matter. Like every boy, I wanted desperately to fit in and be a part of the group. Nobody wants to feel like an outsider. I know I didn't. But what these guys didn't realize is that I had something going for me that protected me from their taunting. I had experience. I had been here before and I had learned something. You can turn any liability into an asset.

It all went back to one Christmas when I was five years old. I wanted a bicycle more than anything else but things around our house were tight. Dad had been injured and off the job for awhile. That's why my Aunt Lucille had compassion on me and gave the treasured machine to my parents to give me for Christmas. And on Christmas morning, there it was. A bike – a blue 20-inch girl's bike. At the time I paid no attention to the gender of the machine. I'm not sure I even knew the difference. I just saw the bicycle of my dreams.

My dad and mom worked the rest of that Christmas day helping me learn how to maneuver the bike without falling on my behind.

It's amazing what parents do for their children. My dad was a blue-collar worker and my mom was a stay at home mom. They gave me time. I can't ever remember complaining, "You never spend time with me." They came to my football games when I wasn't worth a hoot and sometimes I would find myself looking up in the stands and asking, "Why do they come? I never get to play." They came to all my softball games cheering me on and bragging on every little thing I did. Such as my dad saying to the guy sitting next to him, "Have you ever seen a kid who could strike out with such style?" That kind of stuff.

So there was a lot of meaning attached to that bike and I was determined to ride it for the rest of my life. And I did ride it until I finally wore it out. I was about twenty-five at the time of my bike's demise. Bye, bye, little blue bicycle. You and I have been a team for years – kind of like Roy Rogers and Trigger. Except, unlike Roy, I didn't stuff my teammate when it expired.

Now here I am peddling right into the middle of these guys who think they're giving me a hard time. I blurt out, "Hey, guys, watch this!" And I start moving down the street at a blinding speed and just as I've reached top throttle I slam on the brakes and pull that bike up in the air turning it around in midair before hitting the ground again and suddenly peddling in the opposite direction. A big smile starts spreading all the way across my face. I have just shown these guys what you can do when you travel light on a blue 20-inch girl's bike. Try that on your big cumbersome 26 incher!

I know I'm bragging, but I remember hearing some guy say that he who toots not his own horn shall remain in a perpetual state of untootedness. So I was a good bike rider. Toot! I could make that little cycle do all sorts of tricks. Toot! My little girl's peddle brake bicycle could ride circles around their 26-inch hand brake bicycles. Toot! And the rest of the afternoon every one of those boys was begging to ride my bike – yes, my little blue 20-inch girl's bike.

And I let them. And any time I wanted to ride someone's big boy's bike, I got to. Toot!

Gone, but Not Forgotten

Little boys playing in the yard grow up to be big boys going off to war.

The school bell at the old Northport Elementary School rang and I headed home falling in with Donald White as we made our way down the street the short distance to his home on Main Avenue. When we got there I stayed awhile doing what little boys love to do – play and play and play. I forget if the game was cops and robbers or cowboys and Indians or something else. I just remember having a good time with a walk home buddy. I did this over and over.

Donald White was a likeable and friendly guy. He was a favorite of many of his fellow students and all of his teachers. Being a few grades ahead of Don I rarely saw him once I moved to high school and out of the neighborhood. Time passed and we grew up, both graduating from TCHS.

Then one day I picked up my newspaper only to see that Donald White had lost his life in Vietnam. My mind went back to those days of carefree living when we'd walk home together and he'd be the Lone Ranger and I'd be Tonto.

Life is filled with things we can't predict and don't understand. As a boy I remember listening to one of my favorite songs, "Que Sera Sera." I guess the reason I liked it so much was because I was asking the same questions as the singer.

The questions: "What will I be? Will I be handsome, will I be rich? What lies ahead? Will we have rainbows day after day?"

The answer: "Que Sera Sera, whatever will be will be. The future's not ours to see, Que Sera Sera, what will be will be."

Probably every child has questions of that sort. When we're young we want to know what kind of life is ahead of us – What will I be like? What will I do for a living? Whom will I marry? How many children will I have? Where will I live?

These questions have been answered for me. They were never answered for Donald and the more than fifty eight thousand who went off to Vietnam and never came back.

As I said, Don was a congenial fellow. He made friends easily. I can only imagine with his personality and abilities what all he could have accomplished. I think those accomplishments would have been considerable.

Yes, little boys playing in the yard grow up to be young men going off to war. And those who don't, owe a tremendous debt to those who do.

Thank you, Donald White, for giving your life to fight for your country and secure freedom for people at home and a world away. You did us proud. I will try hard not to squander this precious gift bequeathed to us by such a great sacrifice.

VI

The Loves of My Life

My First True Love

IT WAS LOVE AT first sight. No doubt about that. I was visiting my aunt one weekend and happened to be walking through the field across from her house when I saw my dream. She was gorgeous. She was beautiful. She was every boy's fantasy.

Joyce was a tall good-looking brunette who lived down the street from my aunt. My best pal Mickey Nix and I used to tease each other about liking her and she actually wound up marrying Mick. Joyce may have been Mickey's true love but she wasn't the first love I saw that day.

Dawn was a cute and pert little blonde who could make any boy look twice. She lived next door to my aunt and many times I would go out and play in the yard just so I could get a glimpse of her. But neither was Dawn the true love I saw that day.

The great attraction I saw in the field that fateful moment was a first baseman's mitt. That's right, I had fallen in love with a glove. The object of my affection had been lying there for quite some time and was all caked up with dried mud. She had seen her best days because this mitt had no padding and a hole on the backhand side big enough to put three fingers through. But it didn't matter. Just lying there she stole my heart. She called to me. She was irresistible.

I reached down, picked her up, knocked off the mud, put her on my left hand and walked away with my true love firmly in my grasp. I was a happy human being.

My first baseman's mitt, like any true love, was a continuous source of joy and provided me with countless hours of good times. We played and laughed together. Well, I don't know if a glove can laugh but I did. Actually, the first time I showed up at a neighborhood game sporting the beloved mitt I thought Ronnie Davis and his thirteen year old uncle, Terry Whitehead, were going to die laughing. I joined in the fun. I had to agree – it was kind of hilarious, the other guys with their good store bought gloves and me with my padless and holey field found mitt so big it almost fell off my hand.

But it was mine. It was free. And, as I said, it was my first true love.

We boys had a good chuckle at such a sight but then as we started playing ball a strange thing happened. Every boy on the lot wanted to try his hand at wearing my "new" glove. She was the hit of the afternoon. I knew she would be. That's why I could laugh with the fellows.

My glove and I stayed together until her last gasp. I had found her when I was nine and she had been a faithful companion for all those years. But now I was sixteen and my love glove had seen her best days. I knew it and, in a sense, I think she knew it.

When you have had such a good relationship with your baseball glove you can't just toss her in the trash. That would be sacrilege. There was only one thing to do. So on a rainy afternoon I sneaked out to the woods behind our house, dug a hole and buried her.

She deserved a proper funeral and that meant somebody should speak some words over her. I was the only one in sight so I cleared my throat and softly said, "Here lies the best glove a boy could ever hope for. She was a good glove – the best in my opinion. She caught every ball that came her way. Any time I missed it was my fault, not hers. I'm going to miss her but it gives me great comfort knowing that she's going to that great baseball diamond in the sky."

And with that I turned and walked away. And like every person after a funeral I went home and ate fried chicken and potato salad. It's what she would have wanted.

My Puppy Love Bit My Heart

I guess every boy has a puppy love that he remembers fondly. Mine was the girl who lived across the road when I was about twelve. Virginia Henry was her name and she was about ten when I happened to look over her way one day thinking that this gal is as pretty as a picture. And her little sister, Yvonne, was as cute as a button.

So I crossed the road not only to get on the other side but to meet my attractive neighbors. Virginia and I started playing together every day and for a while we were inseparable. Until one day when I did the unthinkable. I hit her in the stomach – with a rock.

I was holding the rock in my hand and teasing her saying, "If you move I'll hit you with this rock." I was giggling inside because I knew what I was up to having devised this trick of dropping the rock behind me and swinging my arm around as if the old rock were still in my hand. It always made the person in front of me flinch. So I thought it was a pretty good joke. Thus the internal giggling.

Only this time the joke was on me. For some reason the rock didn't drop. It stayed in my hand until I swung my arm around letting that rock head straight toward Virginia's tummy. Whop! Umph!

I stood there in shock. She stood there in shock. Even her dog was shocked. Shock waves circled the entire earth. I had done the unthinkable. I had done something I had been taught to never ever do – hit a girl. And now she was hit – from my own hand.

Virginia ran into the house crying and old Billy Boy bolted across the road into the woods behind my house. I just knew her daddy would come looking for me and the police would eventually show up and drag me off in cuffs. I was nervous. I was afraid. I was sorry that I had hurt my best friend. "Please, God, if you'll forgive me and not let her daddy beat me up and if you'll save me from a life-time in jail I'll never do this again."

I'm happy to report that I never did any jail time and her dad never showed up. I finally went back across the road and apologized to Virginia. She didn't throw rocks back at me or ban me from the premises. She just forgave me. That's one thing I liked about her – she didn't hold it against me when I did something stupid.

People used to tease me about my puppy love. I'd go to school and Virginia's cousin, Jerry, would start in on me calling out to me in a sweetie-sweet voice, "Hey, Virginia". I'd get embarrassed and mad at the same time and chase him all over the schoolyard - until one day he outgrew me and started chasing back.

I finally worked up enough nerve to go public and ask Virginia to a party. I remember the night of the big event as we waited by the side of the road looking for Mr. Mitchell to come by and pick us up in his old Studebaker. I still remember what she wore – I have a good memory. She was all decked out in a pretty blue dress. Or was it green? Or yellow? It was hard to tell in the late afternoon shadows. But I know it was a dress. Or was it a pants outfit? It was hard to tell in the late afternoon shadows. One thing I'm sure of – she looked pretty in whatever she was wearing. Shadows or no shadows.

They say that all good things must come to an end. I don't know about that but it was true for our puppy love. There came a day when Virginia and her family moved away. I hate to admit it but I made it a point to stay away from her house on moving day which prompted my mom to ask, "Aren't you going to say good-bye to Virginia and Yvonne?"

I blurted out, "I don't care if they move all the way to Africa!"

But I did care. I was hurting inside. My heart was breaking and my tears were flowing. I hid in the woods watching as they drove away for the last time.

Good-bye, Virginia. Thanks for being my best friend when we were kids.

The Love Bug Bites

I was a thirteen year old kid standing in the back of the Five Points Baptist Church auditorium watching and listening as Margaret Ann Bigham was rehearsing her role as our Youth Sunday song leader. She was getting a sound check when Tommy Poe turned to me and said, "Margaret has such a soft voice." And I agreed, but it wasn't her voice that was getting my attention. It was her bright red hair and beautiful face and gorgeous figure that kept me looking.

I muttered under my breath, "One of these days I'm gonna ask her for a date. One of these days I'm gonna marry that gorgeous gal."

Of course, I had to wait until I grew up to make good on those desires. But I did grow up. And I did make good on what I had promised myself years before.

So one Sunday night after church was over and everybody was making their way out the door, I decided to make my move. When we got out on the porch I sauntered on over close to Margaret and looking this way and that way and being assured that at the moment we were sort of alone I swallowed hard and blurted out, "May I take you home?" The question had kind of stuck in my throat for a brief moment but then I decided that it was now or never.

I never will forget her answer. "No."

I was stunned and crestfallen and my ego started spiraling downward. I had worked up the courage to ask and had rehearsed my approach - and for what? To be turned down?

But I will say this – she rejected me in a soft voice.

I slumped away to my two-tone '53 Ford and headed straight to the Cove Restaurant where I drowned my sorrows with a hot steak sandwich and sweet tea. I felt like saying to the other guys, "Okay, fellows, have another round of sweet tea and this one's on me." That's what you do when you're down. You don't want to drink alone.

What was I to do? Well, you know how Superman gets knocked around by those aliens from outer space but then rallies and with full force wins the day? That's what I did. I rallied. I came back with full force. I won the day. I asked Margaret again and this time she took me up on my offer. So the both of us walked over to my cream and brown two-tone '53 Ford and headed to the Cove where I suddenly discovered that a hot steak sandwich and sweet tea go down a whole lot better when your true love is by your side.

Of course, this was our first outing together and we had not officially fallen in love - but I knew. It was just a matter of time. We may not have known it then, but we had just begun a four year journey that would culminate in our walking the aisle on that twenty-eighth day of June in 1968.

Actually, that first outing was not what we call our first date. It was just a drive home after church and I had popped the question on the front porch of the church in the middle of a crowd. I don't know if that counts as a date. Maybe our true first date was later - a result of my calling her on the phone good and proper and asking her to a banquet. But that also has some problems qualifying as a date because we were accompanied by a half dozen little boys. I was their Royal Ambassador group leader and it was an area wide RA banquet at the Baptist Student Union we were attending. Margaret understood this and so when the car began loading up with nine and ten year old fellows she knew what was going on.

Maybe our first real date was one night after church when I was transporting some of those same RA boys home and Margaret was seated by my side. My intention was to drop off the boys and then go somewhere with my date. I didn't count on it raining cats and dogs and I certainly didn't count on driving that two-tone '53

Ford right into a ditch in the front of Joel French's house. But even bad things can turn out good. The impact of hitting the ditch threw Margaret over against me and for the first time I had a "hello there" encounter. And it felt good.

So there is our date legacy. Now how many people do you know who had three first dates with the same person? If Floyd Cramer had only known he would have titled his song "First Date". That's much more interesting and optimistic than crying about a last date.

Is it possible to love someone with your whole heart in the beginning and then after fifty plus years love that person even more? I mean, if there is all-out love to begin with then how is it possible to increase? Well, I'm not a philosopher and cannot answer that question. I just know that Margaret and I love each other more today than we ever have and I don't see that changing tomorrow or the next day or forever. We're just enjoying it like two love-sick teenagers who have never grown up.

VII

Friends Are Forever

The Mick

LIFE IN THE FIFTIES. You can't beat it. Here is this Northport boy playing baseball across town on the vacant lot next to my Aunt Lucille's house in the Forest Lake area. I'm in the batter's box. Sammy Maze is winding up on the pitcher's mound thinking that he's going to deliver me a pitch that I cannot hit. He then delivers me a pitch that I cannot hit.

Whiff. Strike one! That's okay. I'll get the next one. Whiff. I swing and nothing but air. Still okay. I'm just warming up. I'll hit this next one so far it'll take the FBI to find it. Whiff. Strike three! I've just saved the G-men a whole lot of trouble.

Sammy yells, "You're out!" And he's right if you are playing by the rules. But who wants to play by the rules when you need another swing?

So I make my plea. "C'mon, man. Give me one more shot." Sammy agrees to the extra strike. I know why. He knows I'm not going to hit this one either. And he's right. I don't. Strike four! I throw down my bat complaining as I walk to the outfield, "There's something wrong with this bat! If I had a good bat you'd see what I could do." I'm used to saying that which tells you all you need to know about my batting skills. I have none.

Next up is my friend, Mickey Nix. Mickey is my pal, my buddy, my partner in crime. In other words, my best friend. He lives in the rough and tough Kaulton section of Tuscaloosa where he is the youngest of seven. We were best friends the moment I came into this world a year after Mickey had arrived on the planet. Even our families are best friends and Mickey and I will remain close throughout our boyhood days.

So here's Mickey ready to bat. Sammy spits on the ball. He doesn't know why – he's just heard about some major league pitchers doing it. Anyway, it doesn't help. Whap! Mickey knocks it out of the park. Well, not a park. Just a vacant lot. But there is a row of hedges that's kind of like a fence out in centerfield. So we call it a park.

Mickey really blasts that ball. He is a good athlete. Always. He can run faster, throw farther and jump higher than the rest of us. That's why I sometimes call him The Mick. He reminds me of another fellow who has that nickname – Mickey Mantle, superstar centerfielder for the New York Yankees.

The Mick – Nix, not Mantle – and I meet each other at the Bama Theater for one of those Saturday morning kids' programs. We do this as often as we can. He travels over on the city bus from Kaulton and I travel over from Northport by way of somebody's car.

"Horace, Mom says I can go to the Bama if I can get a ride and since you're going that way anyway I thought I might just hitch one with you." That's me making my pitch to our nineteen year old neighbor. He agrees and now all I have to do is go work on Mom.

"Mom, Horace says he'll be glad to take me to the Bama if it's all right with you." I know I've gotten the cart before the horse, but that's the way I like to travel.

So here I am headed toward a fun morning with several hundred other kids from across the county. We settle in for a morning of watching Roadrunner outsmart the ever innovative Wyle Coyote followed by a giddy up galloping western with Roy Rogers and gang whipping up on the bad guys. We laugh and clap and hoot and yell for about three solid hours.

In between the cartoon and the movie some guy comes out on stage accompanied by a pretty lady. They have a box full of neat prizes and a hat from which the lady starts pulling ticket stubs. She calls out number after number.

In all the years I've been here I've never had my number called. I've never had to get up out of my seat and walk across the stage and claim my prize. But today is different. Today she calls my number.

In all my years I've been here I've never arrived with a hole in the seat of my pants. I've never left the house without Mom's last minute inspection to see if I have a clean neck and decent underwear. But this time somehow the hole and I sneaked by. I guess Mom was so interested in the inner garment she forgot to check the outer duds. I guess she thinks her son has enough sense to not wear pants with a big wide hole right in the sit down place. I guess she was assuming too much. And I guess I was so excited that I just tossed on whatever was hanging on the bed post.

I'm in a panic. The number has been called and the man is waiting. The moments tick by as my window of opportunity is fleeting. I've hesitated long enough so I lean over and whisper in Mickey's ear, "That's my number they're calling but I have a problem. I've got a sizable hole in my pants that shows my underwear. What am I going to do?"

Mick has the solution. "Let's go. I'll stay behind you and hide that hole. Nobody will ever see it." So we both walk across that stage in lock step that would make a drill team proud.

Well, of course, that's what friends are for – to hide holes in your britches. So I get my prize, thanks to my best friend. It's a 45 record of Jerry Lee Lewis singing "Great balls of Fire." And the flip side is an extra bonus being one of my favorites - "You Win Again." And I go home and listen to that piano playing talent sing and play those songs for the next thirty years.

And I'm thinking what a great thing it is to have a friend who will cover your rear end.

Thrill Seeking

It was a cold Monday morning before school and we guys were huddled around a big trash can

warming ourselves by the makeshift fire and sharing our weekend stories before entering the halls of learning. Richard was all keyed up about his Saturday and Sunday experience. "Man, I got drunk. Wow! What a time! I drank I don't know how many beers and got sick as a dog and threw up all over the place. I was really bombed out of my skull! Man!"

He said it like it was a good thing. But I was not impressed and Richard picked up on my negative vibes about his positive enthusiasm so he asked me, "Man, haven't you ever gotten drunk?" and when I said that I had not he exclaimed, "Man, you don't know what you're missing!"

I said, "Yes I do. You just told me – getting sick as a dog and throwing up all over the place and being bombed out of my skull." Why anybody would question my sanity for not particularly caring to have such an experience was beyond me but Richard just looked at me like I was from another planet. And for the record, I'm from planet earth and have been far as long as I can remember.

I've just always had a revulsion to anything alcohol. Maybe that all started one day up on my grandpa's farm. I was about thirteen and since I grew up in a teetotaler household I had never had any experience with the old joy juice. But my uncle had made some homemade muscadine wine and one day I sneaked out to the smokehouse where the firewater was hidden. I guess I was motivated by the desire to just do something forbidden but I also wanted to see what the allure of an alcoholic drink was all about. I would just take a swig and see for myself.

I found the jug of squeezings and chugged it down. Then I chucked it up. My drinking career was over before it ever started and to this day I have never drunk anything stronger than root beer - if you exclude that eighty percent alcohol cough medicine I swallowed one time. By the way, it didn't cure my cough but I didn't care.

My absolute refusal to imbibe has at times caused me to be out of sync with some of my friends. But early on I learned that I didn't have to go along with everything my buddies did for them to be my buddies. Which is why I have friends on both ends of the drinking spectrum whom I dearly love and whose company I thoroughly enjoy. I don't pester those who indulge and they don't make fun of my abstinence. And I have the good sense to stay away from those who do indulge while they're under the influence.

Like all other teens I was looking for excitement and thrills and a good time. I just chose other ways to get those thrills - some of them good and some not so good. One of the good ones was stuffing a whole bunch of guys and gals into a car and heading out to Alberta City to cruise over thrill hill.

The place is famous around these parts. You drive along one of the side streets and come over a hill where the bottom of the road suddenly falls out from under you and you think you're going into a free fall. It's pandemonium inside the car with everybody screaming like they've just seen the scariest scene in the scariest movie ever. It enhances the fun if you have some world class screamers with you and since Peggy Poe and Sandra Winters were the two best screamers in the universe I tried to make sure that they were along when heading to thrill hill. And if we wanted to double our pleasure we'd talk Billy Jones into driving us in his super loud '56 Ford. Screams and gutted mufflers and a steep hill that scares the stuffing out of you – it doesn't get any better than that!

After going over the famous hill a few more times and being assured the screamers were all screamed out we'd head back to Frank Lary's Tastee Freeze in Northport and have us a tiger burger and some fries and a delicious milkshake. And I would wake up the next morning, not bombed out of my skull, but remembering it all.

Smoke-Out

Puff… hack…cough. That's what I was doing in the cab – not a taxi cab, but the cab of Donald Hamner's truck.

I was spending the week with my Uncle Thomas Smelley (only two years my senior even though he was my mother's brother). On Sunday night Donald picked up Thomas and me in his truck to go to church. And we did go. Drove right up to the front of Mt. Olive Baptist Church.

Here's the church and there's the steeple but we never opened the door to see all the people.

Donald looked over at the two of us and asked, "Do ya'll want to go to church or ride around?"

Well, I don't think any of us was feeling too religious that night so we voted 3-0 to ride. I knew it was wrong and I really didn't mean to be an out and out pagan, but I thought it might be fun. And it was. Sin is always fun. If it wasn't nobody would ever do it.

We drove all over the northern part of the county on roads I had never seen before.

After we got out of sight of the church Donald pulled out some cigars. Donald took one. Thomas took one. I took one. Thomas lit up. Donald lit up. I just sat there.

"Aren't you going to light up?" I sat there thinking how it was going to be hard enough explaining this skipping church business without having to add cigar smoking to my list of transgressions, too. I could visualize not being able to sit down for a couple of weeks. And my rear end could do more than visualize.

"Nah, I'm going to save mine and smoke it next week." I didn't let on that I really never intended to smoke that cigar because of an experience I had had one day not too long before that – out behind my grandpa's barn. I had smuggled some cigarettes from somewhere and thought I would see what the delight was all about. I lit up and turned every shade of green in the color spectrum and began to feel woozy. What people see in this noxious weed I'll never know. I swore off smoking forever. And now here I was in the presence of two world-class smokers urging me to indulge. How could I tell them this was no fun for me?

"Hey, Thomas, when we get back to the house Papa (my grandfather) and Mizz Cora (the only grandmother I ever knew) will smell the smoke and we'll be in trouble. They'll send me home and I won't get to spend the whole week with you."

Donald broke in, "We've got that one figured out. After we smoke these cigars we'll chew gum and they'll never know." I offered up more reasons for the smoking ban and they came up with more ways to get around those excuses. You could tell these guys had earned extra credit from excuse making school.

So I finally decided to tell them the truth. "I don't care for smoking."

Why didn't I say that in the first place? They were okay with it. But I really might as well have lit up anyway because pretty soon the whole truck was filled with the aroma of cigar tobacco. How is chewing gum going to get this out of my clothes? That thought was rolling through my mind as we proceeded to play smoke-out. Roll up the windows and fill the vehicle with smoke and see who is the first one who goes for the window.

Guess who was the first one to go for the window? I cried out, "Roll the windows down!"

"Nah, not yet. Hang in there little buddy."

But I got my wish when I added, "Okay, if you want puke all over the inside of your truck!" Windows came flying down.

Back at the house we stayed our distance from Papa and Mizz Cora so they wouldn't smell the smoke. We had dodged a bullet. Then Mizz Cora just had to ask, "What did the preacher preach on?" I found out that night that it's not enough just to say he preached on sin. It may have worked for Calvin Coolidge, but it didn't work for us.

Skinny Dipping in February

Okay, here is a story that I have debated with myself whether or not to tell. Among me, myself and I the first vote was 2-1 not to tell. Then after much discussion with me and myself there was another vote that went 2-1 for telling. So although it was never unanimous, here it is.

One cold day in early February I'm walking through the woods on my granddaddy's land with my Uncle Thomas Smelley, my cousin Douglas Holloway and our good friend Donald Hamner. We are messing around and like all teenage boys everywhere looking for something fun to do.

We come upon a creek flowing though these woods and someone makes the suggestion that we go swimming. I'm not too sure about this because it's cold and besides, we don't have any swimsuits. But I do discover that day that birthday suits are perfect for swimming. So we strip down to our altogether and jump into the icy water.

After splashing around for awhile – just the four of us – we hear noises. "Someone's coming through the woods!" says our lookout. Everybody's ready to run for cover until we see that there are more guys with the same crazy idea and before we know it that little creek is covered with just about every boy in the northern part of the county.

And they have all brought their birthday suits so we have total participation. Which proves that the insanity of going swimming in the buff in cold February is not unique to our little circle, but is an affliction that strikes the whole male gender. I find great comfort in that fact because I don't want to be stupid by myself.

The creek is way too shallow for me to do my famous cannon ball dive but be that as it may we have a ton of fun and we're okay as long as we keep moving. The worst thing about it all is standing outside the water dripping dry before putting our clothes back on. But we survive and leave invigorated and ready for our next adventure.

One of those is at another swimming hole. This one is a little different – no creek, no woods and no swimsuits of the birthday kind. I'm talking about the Queen City Park pool. I love this place and come here as often as I can.

So I'm up on the high dive because my friends have said that I'm too chicken to plunge in from that height. I prove them wrong. Yes, I am chicken but I prove that even a scared bird can do a cannon ball off the old stratosphere board. Water splashes everywhere and one woman looks at me as if to say – You got water on my nice new bathing suit. And I return the look as if to say – Why in the world did you come to a swimming pool if you don't want to get wet? And then I catch a glimpse of her muscle-bound boyfriend so I change my look as if to say – Hi there, nice day and no, I won't ever do that again.

But I do it again. Not there. But at Smith Creek where I join a lot of my friends and we splash to our hearts' content in that creek that runs through the pasture land of Flatwoods. Earl Mitchell is there. So is Lloyd Junkin and David Lewis and Curtis Ramsey and Bunky Williams and me, of course. And a whole lot more but if I list them all it will take more space than the editors allow me. We're just a bunch of boys doing what boys love to do in the old summertime – jumping and diving and swimming and having the time of our lives.

Somebody in our group yells, "Snake!" and everybody clears out as we stand on the bank and watch that slimy creature swim out of the water and slither away into the woods. We're about to call it quits (who wants to swim with the snakes) until someone (I think it was Earl because he was always the spokesman for the group) brings us back to our senses by saying, "This is crazy. A few minutes ago we were swimming with the snake in the water and now that he's out of the water we're not getting back into the water. That doesn't make sense!"

So we get back in hoping that Mr. Snake has no cousins nearby. Because if he does, we'll take our business elsewhere. Or do our business right there.

Brothers and Others

I grew up without any brothers although I understand that both of my sisters have one. I always thought it would be a lot of fun having a brother, so early on I went in search of such an animal. And I found him. Over two hundred miles separate us and even though nowadays we rarely get to see each other we have still been as close as brothers since the day we met.

I'm talking about Sam Jones. He grew up with the nickname Billy, but once he ventured out into the world beyond home he started using the Sam name. And that makes sense in a lot of ways. One, it is his real name. And two, both of his grandpas bore that name so it's a way to keep the Sam heritage going. And three, another Sam Jones – a Methodist preacher in olden times - was a hero to Sam.

Sam used to tell me stories about that Reverend Sam Jones of yesteryear. Such as the time the elder Sam was traveling through some isolated woods and was accosted by a man who threatened him with life and limb. Reverend Sam asked the would-be villain if he could pray before the guy did him in. And without waiting for an answer Sam got off his horse and dropped to his knees and said something like this: "Lord, you know I'm your servant and I thank you for protecting me from all these robbers and murderers over the years. Now this man here intends me harm and I know what you usually do in such a circumstance. So I beg of you, please don't kill this man like you did those others. Please don't make this man drop dead on the spot. Spare his life, O Lord." When the Reverend opened his eyes the murderous thief was nowhere to be seen.

I can understand Sam wanting to identify with such a colorful character because the Sam Jones I know is quite a colorful character in his own right.

We used to pal around for hours discussing things we knew something about and some we didn't. Which never stopped us from pontificating on any subject you care to mention. We also did things together, again, some we knew something about and some we didn't. Such as dating.

One afternoon we had a meeting to discuss some important business. The subject was girls and that's about as important as it gets for teenage boys. Somewhere in this meeting Sam made a motion. "Hey, let's double date this Saturday night?" I seconded the motion and after a little discussion the motion passed. Unanimously.

Of course, now we had to decide who to ask and I distinctly remember the one major requirement – they had to look good. So we chose a couple of gorgeous girls to carry putt-putt golfing.

Now Sam and I may not have been the brightest bulbs on the planet but neither were we the dimmest. But this decision was toward the dim end of the spectrum because we didn't have enough sense to date someone we could beat at golf. Guys are supposed to be macho. Guys are supposed to win in any competition with gals. But the girls creamed us. Of course, what you do when you lose to a girl is come up with an excuse and we've got one. We were simply distracted by their beauty and everybody knows how hard it is to hit a ball straight when you're distracted.

I can assure you that the girls did not have a similar problem. But there's no need to get into a discussion about that.

Life is funny. There are twists and turns that surprise you. On that double date Margaret Ann Bigham was Sam's date and Shelia Burroughs was mine (Sorry, Shelia, for letting the world know that you ever dated the likes of me, but everyone has a skeleton or two in her past).

It's ironic that the first date I had with my future wife was not with my future wife. I had always wanted to date Margaret but I fooled around so long that I let Sam edge me out. However, I guess that double date was the impetus I needed to stop messing around so soon afterwards I somehow managed to finagle a date with this redheaded beauty and like they say, the rest is history.

You would have thought that I had learned my lesson about carrying a girl on a date that involved sports skill. But I'm a slow learner. Not long after that golf shellacking Margaret and I went on a date and I experienced a bowling shellacking.

How that happened I don't know. I mean I bowled with a sixteen pound ball and she with a twelve. I slung it down the alley with furious force and she with a little nudge. I was bigger. I was stronger. I was the guy, she was the gal. But all that was for nothing as she kept piling up the strikes while I was cleaning out the gutters. Those gutters at Leland Lanes have never been more spick and span which almost prompted me to work up a little deal with the manager. If he would give me free passes I'd come by every few days and clean the gutters for him.

I will say in my defense that Margaret had taken bowling in a PE class at UA so I didn't know that I was competing with a professional. That wouldn't have happened if we had been dating in today's world. I could have simply gone on facebook and checked out her life resume.

Well, while I was moving on in my relationship with Margaret, Sam moved on to South Alabama and started looking for his love across the state line in Mississippi. A young and talented beauty named Laura Fisher helped him along.

You may wonder where Shelia was in all this dating intrigue. I mean she was and still is a very gorgeous girl and I always enjoyed being around her. Let's just say that she had the good sense to marry someone with good sense. And as things developed she and Jerry Baggett walked the aisle exactly two weeks before Margaret and I did. Because of that I can always remember their anniversary so that if Jerry ever forgets that important date I can help him out.

You don't have to watch the Hallmark romance channel to get your story with a happy ending. You can get it right here. I found my life love and Sam found his and Shelia and Margaret found theirs. And we have all lived happily ever after. Let them make a movie about that. We're available.

VIII

The Church I Grew Up In

Armour's One-Man Harmonica Band

OKAY HERE I AM at a sixties' youth party and ready to make an impression on my fellow teenagers. After all, what good is a party if you can't be the center of attention every now and then? I have brought my trusty harmonica and am looking for an opportunity to show off my musical skill on this old mouth instrument. So I pull it out, bounce it on my pants to shake out all the germs and begin to blow. Let the party begin!

I've been practicing for weeks on the only song I know how to play. It is my own rendition of "Heaven Bound Train", an instrumental made famous by the Southern Gospel group, The Lefevres. With cheeks puffing and eyes bulging I'm blowing that old French harp for all it's worth while this very active and boisterous crowd picks up the rhythm and accompanies me with clapping of hands and stomping of feet. It's a very festive piece of music and the crowd is in the mood and I'm not doing too badly even if I say so myself. At least I'm making a lot of noise. And noise is the name of the game at a youth party.

Now some people may be surprised because I'm basically an introvert and what causes me to do front and center things every now and then is hard to explain. I mostly like being to myself even though I never have had a problem putting myself out there if I think the circumstances call for it.

For example, one day I'm sitting there in my college classroom of about two hundred students. Now remember, I'm shy. I'm reserved. I like my anonymity. But the professor says something that needs further clarification. So my hand shoots up and for the next minute I forget about all those other students in the auditorium. I know it's crazy. I'm an introvert, for goodness sake. I'm not supposed to speak in public. But such is my introvertness (a word I just made up) that some of my extrovertness (another of my creations) comes bursting out. Maybe we ought to stop putting people into categories and just say, "Hey, you're just you. And that's okay."

Now remember, I'm playing this harmonica in front of the youth crowd when all of a sudden it's over. I have played my tune and we've stomped and clapped and now we're done. We can now proceed to the refreshment table where the hot dogs and chili bowls await us.

But that's before Armour.

You know how in a football game the momentum can change in the batting of an eyelash. Well, I find out this night that the same can happen with attention. Because the attention is about to swing from me to someone in the crowd that no one would suspect of being a charismatic super talent. I'm talking about Armour Freeman, one of our youth teachers and one of the best men I have ever known, who, as soon as I finish my masterpiece, asks if he can borrow my harmonica for a minute. He bounces it on his pants to shake out all the germs (which is something I'm beginning to think all harmonica players do) and puts it to his mouth and begins to blow.

And for the next few minutes we hear what we've never heard before.

Armour blows that mouth machine like he's at the Grand Ole Opry on a Saturday night. As a matter of fact I don't think I've ever heard anybody on the Opry do it as well. Here he is blowing that mouth harp every which way known to man. He blows it right and left, up and down, in and out, north and south, east and west. He blows it up in the hills and down in the valley. He blows it over the ocean and around the desert and back to the ocean again. He's here, he's there, he's everywhere with that mouth piece. He's getting sounds out of that little old cheap French harp that I never thought possible.

After bringing down the house and making the place rock Armour hands the harmonica back to me. And it's smoking. It's hot. It's the same old harmonica I handed him earlier but it has been transformed into a classic. I'm ready to put that music machine in a glass case and send it to the Country Music Hall of Fame in Nashville.

But I don't. I simply go back home and practice on it looking for the day when I can play as well as Armour. So far I haven't made it. But I do still have that amazing harmonica put up in a case and for a couple of bucks I'll let you see it. And I'll take it out of that case and bring it to your party for a tune or two – if your party is hard of hearing. If they're not, you'll have to ask Armour to play.

Mr. Rover Goes to Church

I am sitting on the platform nervously looking over the congregation. In a few minutes I will be standing before these people preaching a sermon I have been working on ever since our pastor, David W. Lewis, had asked me to fill in for him so he could take a few days off. I am only a teenager and know what all teens know – everything and nothing. One is what I think I know and the other is what I actually know. It will take me years before bringing these two closer together.

My dad is leading the singing this night so I know the pump will be primed when I get up to deliver my message. Dad has a gift for getting a congregation to sing their best.

So visualize what's going on at this point. The ushers are down front ready to pass the offering plates once the prayer is said and Dad is standing behind the podium ready to sing the offertory once the man doing the praying is done. All across the auditorium eyes are closed and heads are bowed.

Except mine.

It is kind of a long prayer that starts reverently enough as the "brother" is invoking the Almighty. But then I begin to hear some heavy breathing getting closer and closer to me. I know it isn't my dad because he's in terrific shape and never seems to be out of energy.

Now I know you're not supposed to do this and I teach children to keep their eyes shut during the entire prayer but I can't resist opening my eyes to see the source of this heavy breathing. And when I open my peepers I find myself face to face with a big old blue-tick hound dog. Someone has left the side door open and Mr. Rover, apparently wanting to set a good example for all the neighborhood pups, decides to come in for a night of praise and celebration.

I think – I can't believe I'm up here in this pulpit face to face with Curtis Ramsay's old hound dog. Or somebody's. I do the only thing I know to do in such a situation – close my eyes and send up a quick prayer. A specific prayer – "Lord, please make this animal go away!"

Right there that night on that stage in that moment of time I experience the anguish of unanswered prayer. For when I open my eyes again I see Mr. Rover still faithfully occupying my part of the platform and staring straight at me as if to say, "Hi ya, Billy, got a good one for us tonight?"

Now every preacher has to deal with some things before he gets up to preach - maybe the jitters or maybe some feeling of unworthiness or maybe a sore throat that he's been fighting for several days or maybe one of the straps on his suspenders has suddenly popped and turned loose. None of that for me. This night my pre-sermon problem is dealing with a hound dog.

All kinds of thoughts are racing through my mind. If that mutt is still here when I get up to preach what will the people think? What will they say? Will they get the idea that I brought this mongrel in for an object lesson? After all, we have precedent for such a sight and sound sermon.

Glen Courtney, sometime before, had set a basket on fire. Well, he didn't mean to - he was just trying to illustrate the point that we should not hide our light under a bushel, as the Bible says, and so Glen lit a candle and placed it under the basket he had brought. Next thing we knew he had a four alarm fire going.

I had wondered what I could do to top Glen but I never counted on using Rover as an object lesson. Of course, there is a verse in the Bible that says "Beware of dogs." If I am quick on my feet I can possibly work old Rover into my sermon. But right now I'm too concerned about what to do once this prayer is over.

Not to worry. On the heels of the "amen" Dad turns around and noticing the dog in the pulpit grabs that mongrel by the nape of the neck and heads toward the exit. A loud yelp reverberates throughout the building (may be the dog, may be me) and in a jiffy Dad strides back into the pulpit and without missing a beat says, "Now let's sing hymn 216."

Well, I shouldn't have worried so much. Everything worked out fine and after the service several people are so kindly telling me how much they have enjoyed the message. Except one smart aleck. "I guess the preaching in this church is going to the dogs."

In case you're wondering about my reaction to that I have to tell you that I'm still looking for that man and when I find him I'm going to sic Curtis Ramsay's blue-tick hound on him.

Fun in the Old Sunday School Class

It was Sunday morning at 9:30 and I was where I was every Sunday at that time – in my Sunday school class of nine and ten year old boys and girls ready to listen to our teacher, Mr. Victor Mitchell, tell us about the Bible. The class secretary was calling the roll and we were answering, not with a simple "here" or "present", but with a Bible verse. We were getting a head start on our Bible study because answering roll with a quote was a requirement that Mr. Mitchell had placed on the roll calling exercise.

You could be sure that the first kid would answer with "Jesus wept". That's John 11:35(KJV), the shortest verse in the Bible. And the next one that was sure to go was John 3:16, the most familiar verse in the Bible. Most kids who grow up in the Bible Belt can quote the John verse in its entirety as soon as they can talk.

After those two easy verses the challenge was on. We had to come up with a Bible quote that was more extensive and less familiar.

And so it went every Sunday until Bunky Williams came up with another two word verse – "Rejoice evermore" – I Thessalonians 5:16 (KJV). That surprised everyone in the room and we all wondered how many hours old Bunk had pored over the Scriptures before digging up that gem. That sent some more of us Bible-quoting pupils searching for shorter verses.

Hey, here's one – only three words – "Pray without ceasing"- I Thessalonians 5:17 (KJV). And another – "Despise not prophesyings" – I Thessalnoians 5:20 (KJV). And another – "Brethren, pray for us." – I Thessalonians 5:25 (KJV). Okay, that has four words but still short enough to quote at roll call without pumping up our anxiety factor.

This roll call business was beginning to get interesting. One day one of the guys came up with this beauty – "At Parbar westward, four at the causeway, and two at Parbar." I Chronicles 26:18 – I Chronicles 26:18 (KJV). Not all that short, but interesting. That challenged everybody else to search the scriptures during the week and see if we could top last week's offerings. So one Sunday somebody came in with this gem from the book of Proverbs – "It is better to dwell in the corner of a housetop than with a brawling woman in a wide house." – Proverbs 21:9 (KJV).

We thought we were so smart. But Mr. Mitchell was way ahead of us. He thought that if we were going to choose a verse just for its brevity or obscurity or entertainment factor he would start asking for the meaning of the verse.

"Billy, what does that verse about the brawling woman mean?" I thought I knew but was afraid to say it. Mr. Mitchell smiled and answered for me, "Be careful who you marry." He said it with a wink in his eye and a smile on his face. And I shut my eyes trying to visualize a wild-eyed woman grabbing and flinging everything in sight – including her husband - all over the house. Which is why I eventually married a woman who was not so wild. I didn't want to live in the attic. I've stayed in the dog house a few times but never the attic.

We got quite an education just answering the roll call. I guess that was the whole purpose.

But there was more to Sunday school than just answering roll. There was friendly competition. Every Sunday we counted heads to see who had the most there – boys or girls. It was a big deal to us so imagine how elated we guys felt one day after all heads were counted and the boys outnumbered the girls - by one. Of course we were counting Mr. Mitchell on the guy side.

Here we were rubbing it in, "Yaa, yaa, we got more than ya'll! Yuk yuk!"

Suddenly Mr. Mitchell threw a monkey wrench into the machinery, so to speak, putting a damper on our celebration. "Count me as a girl today."

Wait a minute! This is going to swing the victory to the other side. Is this legal?

Lonnie Ramsey couldn't stand it, blurting out, "Well, I've never seen a bald-headed girl before." The whole class roared.

But all Mr. Mitchell did was smile, rub his hairless head and say, "Well, you have now." He didn't mind being a bald-headed girl if the girls needed him to be.

We kids loved it. We loved him. And of course, he loved all his kids. Yessiree, it was fun in Sunday school. Because it's always fun being around people who love you and let you have a little fun.

What I Learned at Camp

We Baptists have a mission organization for boys called Royal Ambassadors. And every summer there is a big RA camp for boys all across the state. One year Mr. Victor Mitchell drove his son Earl and me all the way to Shocco Springs near Talledega so we could enjoy the RA camping experience.

Earl and I settle in to our cabin when suddenly we hear a commotion outside. Earl runs and flings open the door to find a crowd gathered around two boys swinging at each other. Earl yells in his loudest voice, "Hey, you guys, stop it! This is a Christian camp! We don't do stuff like that here!" He gets right in the middle of them and sternly says, "Now stop fighting and shake hands and don't ever do this again at Shocco Springs!"

No sooner has he said it than the fighting ceases. Right then. Something about the way Earl says it. Something about the look in his eyes and the sound of his voice. Something about the fact that he is twice the size of each of these sluggers. They apologize and shake hands and the two boys who had been fighting go away as pals. What magic Earl has performed!

A few hours later I'm in the cabin by myself when I hear the same sound of commotion again. I decide to do the Earl thing. So I run out the door. Just like Earl. I yell in my loudest voice, "Hey, you guys, stop it! This is a Christian camp! We don't do stuff like that here!" Just like Earl. I get in the middle of them. Just like Earl. Suddenly I'm on the ground with both boys on top of me. Not like Earl. I think – where is Earl when you need him?

That wasn't the only time I was put on the ground. The first day of camp I was running like crazy and halfway down the hill I stopped running and started falling. My body kept moving but without my cooperation. My two feet had tripped over each other and I was sliding downhill with my hand pinned underneath my body scraping over that rocky Talladega turf. It was so bad that I had to go to the camp hospital.

What a way to start my first week of RA camp! But it wasn't all bad. The camp nurse was a very pretty young lady who seemed genuinely interested in me.

"Why were you running down the hill so fast?" She was assuming that speed had caused my fall. Well, in this case she was right but what she didn't know is that I could have been going at a snail's pace and still have fallen. I wouldn't exactly call myself clumsy but Ted Stephens, my neighbor, used to call me feather foot because every time I went to the river with him and tried to get in the boat my feet inevitably slipped and headed toward the water. I was the only boy at the river who went swimming with his shoes on.

"Well, I guess I was in a hurry to get a coke." I was explaining my accident to the pretty nurse.

"You must have wanted one awfully bad," she said.

I did. Every boy in camp did. The camp store was selling these giant twenty-six ounce cokes. Not huge by today's standard but this was in the day of regular six and a half ounce coke bottles. And it was the goal of every boy to get one of these larger versions of the cola and swig it down in world record time.

My folks sent me to camp to learn something. And I did. I learned wisdom. Don't try to break up a fight unless you're as big as Earl Mitchell. I learned patience. If you don't slow down you might not get a chance to swig the big coke. And I learned grace. That was the nurse's name.

Gold Star Mother, All Star Son

I never knew William Mitchell, but I knew his family well – his parents, Victor and Estelle, his siblings, Earl, Elleen, Moody, Maxie, Sarah, and Alfred. William enlisted in the Army Air Corps during World War II and at the young age of eighteen lost his life when his plane was shot down somewhere in Austria. He was tailgunner on a B24 Liberator. William went down with ten other crew members and was buried somewhere in that country until the Army Grave Resurrection crew went to Austria and relocated their remains to the Jefferson Barracks Cemetery in St. Louis.

On the day William's family was notified, his thirteen year old brother, Alfred, was working with Western Union delivering telegrams. When the message came over the wire that William was missing in action the woman in charge promptly sent Alfred home telling him that his day was completed. She then delivered that telegram herself – an act of compassion because she didn't want Alfred delivering the telegram about his own brother.

What an unselfish sacrifice William Mitchell made for his country. What a heartrending sacrifice his mom and dad made as well. I will forever love and respect these people.

I grew up in the shadow of the Mitchell home. They were kind of like an extended family to me. Earl and I were good pals and Elleen was one of my sister's closest friends. I romped and played all over the Mitchell spread and put my feet under their table many times. Earl even taught me how to milk a cow if you can call what I did to old Bessie milking.

All those years I knew that Estelle Mitchell was one of the busiest people I have ever known. She not only raised a family of seven children but was quite active in serving her church and community – for instance, logging over thirteen hundred hours volunteering at the VA. She went all those places and did all those things and never drove a car in her life. I guess that means that Mr. Victor and the rest of the family did a lot of road work getting her to where she needed to be. Thanks are due the entire family for their part in service to the community.

You could say that Victor and Estelle got together by accident. Well, at least their first date was not planned. He showed up ready to take Estelle's sister, Evelyn, on a date but since she was busy washing dishes he opted for Estelle (which makes a case for teenage girls not doing the dishes) and as they say, the rest is history. They tied the knot when he was thirty and she was a mere eighteen. Well, he explained it this way – "I wanted to raise her myself." He always said it with a chuckle and a smile and I'm thinking, "Mr. Victor, you did a good job."

For many years I did not know about William since he died before I was born. I knew that Mrs. Mitchell was a Gold Star Mother but I just thought that was another of the many charitable organizations she was involved with. Then one day my mom explained to me that a Gold Star Mother is a woman who has lost a child in service of the United States Armed Forces. When I heard that I tried to wrap my mind around what it must be like to send a son off to war and get the terrible news that he is not coming back. Of course, you can never understand that unless you have been there yourself.

So every Memorial Day I'm thanking God for people like William Mitchell who gave the big sacrifice, who forfeited his opportunity to grow up and do all the things that people do with their lives – falling in love, getting married, raising a family, enjoying friends – things that he never got to experience because when duty called he answered. I'm also thanking God for Gold Star Mothers like Estelle Mitchell who experience the heartache of sending a son off to war and never seeing him return then somehow transform that heartache into a mammoth amount of service to community and church.

The next time you pass a war memorial or see a U. S. flag waving in the breeze or hear the Star Spangled Banner coming through the air think about Estelle and her son, William, and all those people who gave their all so that you and I can enjoy life, liberty and the pursuit of happiness. And be proud to be an American living in the land of the free and the home of the brave.

IX

Home Sweet Home

My Dad

THERE WE WERE SITTING in the den having a good family time when suddenly the phone rang. I picked it up and some fellow wanted to know if this was where Leroy Gray lived. I said, "Yes, he's my dad."

"Well, may I speak with him?"

Of course, he could. We got calls all the time from anybody and everybody since my dad had become a member of the Northport City Council and we never screened them or tried to put off the callers. If you called, you got an answer. It was as simple as that.

But I could tell that with this particular call something was up. The guy was definitely irritated and ready to bawl out my dad about something. So as I handed the phone over I got close enough to hear the other end of the conversation which was not hard to do since the caller was turning up the volume with every word.

My dad received calls all the time. Late at night or in the middle of supper someone would call and want him to come look at their ditch or something. And Dad never seemed to mind. He loved this kind of stuff although I'll never know why.

But, to tell the truth, this one was too much. I snatched the phone from Dad and said in a tone that matched the caller's for belligerence, "Look here, you bozo, my dad works hard and tries to do the right thing but you yahoos keep calling him and complaining about this and that and can never seem to be satisfied no matter what he does so why don't you just hang up and crawl back into your lair and make everyone happy and just stay there."

You could tell I was not into public relations.

Actually, there is something you should know. I didn't snatch the phone from Dad's hand. If I had, I wouldn't have been able to sit down for a week. And I didn't tell this caller what I thought. Again, if I had, I wouldn't have been able to sit for two weeks. And I certainly didn't call anyone a bozo. That would have added a lifetime of not being able to sit anywhere except on one of those soft cushions that that they give you after you've had hemorrhoid surgery.

So I didn't say anything. But I wanted to. However, Dad took it all in stride. I never heard him get upset with people who were upset with him. He was such a congenial guy and really loved serving people and doing what he could.

Everybody loved Dad. Well, with the exception of an irate caller now and then. It made me feel good that people liked him because when you're a kid and look up to your dad it sure is nice to know that people think highly of him.

It tore my heart out when Dad lost his life in an auto accident on Christmas Eve of 1976. Our friend, Ted Stephens, came into the store where I was working and asked Margaret and me to step outside so he could show us something. Then as we rounded the corner he put his arms around the both of us and said, "I've got some bad news for you kids." And he proceeded to give us the news that would hit me right in the pit of my stomach. Later, I felt sorry for Ted having to deliver such bad news but I have always been grateful that it came from such a dear friend.

I went home that day and just sat there in the den staring into space. I couldn't believe it. And every once in awhile I'd pick up this little puzzle off the coffee table and think of the day my dad brought me that little gadget from a convenience store because he knew I would get a big kick out of a grown man presenting a fifty-nine cent toy to another grown man. He was right. I thought it was hilarious.

Over the years I've had a good chuckle every time I have picked up that puzzle and tried to roll those little balls into the tiny grooves. It was the gift that kept on giving. Playing with that cheap toy was part of my daily ritual until I wore it out. A fifty-nine cent item became one of my favorite possessions.

Silly, huh? But not to me. It was sentimental. It was one of the last things Dad gave me.

If I were to describe my dad I could choose several words. Hardworking is one. He labored as much as any man I have ever known. He thought nothing of putting in a shift at the paper mill and coming home and loading the garden tools and me in our car and heading up to the country to work the little plot of land on my granddaddy's land.

While he was working for the Gulf States Paper Corporation he was also the music director at the Five Points Baptist Church and sold Woodmen of the World insurance as another side job. And somehow he managed to find the time to serve on the Northport City Council for eight years. I can tell you that his days off were never spent in leisure because he was always working around the house or helping someone else. He put in all that sweat time to provide for his family which is something I don't think I fully appreciated until I was older.

Fun is another word that describes my dad. My mind goes back to when I was about seventeen and there we were – father and son - in downtown Tuscaloosa right in front of the courthouse waiting for the light to change. Suddenly I noticed the guy walking across the street in front of us. It was none other than Lee Roy Jordan, the greatest linebacker in college football history. The Bear said about this player, "If they stay in the stadium, Lee Roy will get'em".

I told Dad, "There goes Lee Roy Jordan."

Daddy asked, "Are you sure?" Of course I was. So this man who was my mother's husband hung halfway out the window and yelled loud enough for everyone in town to hear, "Hey, Lee Roy! Roll Tide!" It was Leroy to Lee Roy with both men smiling and waving.

If only the linebacker had known my dad's name he could have yelled, "Back at you, Leroy!" The spelling may be different but the pronunciation is the same.

Later we were sitting around the house talking about the Bama linebacker and Mom said that Dad's name should have been spelled the same way as Lee Roy Jordan's. She said as it is L-e-r-o-y should be pronounced Luh-roy with the emphasis on the last syllable. I said, "You mean like a French name?" and we all got tickled thinking of our dad as a Frenchman while Dad started talking in his best French accent and I'm sitting there thinking of Charles Boyer.

That was Dad. He could turn any ordinary comment into an opportunity to do something funny. Conversations around our house were never boring.

Caring is another word that describes my dad. One day he got to thinking about the homebound - those people who were stuck in their homes day after day seeing only the four walls around them.

"Hey, Billy, what are you doing this afternoon?" Dad wanted to know.

"Not much." I was an active teenager living a pretty full life of school and sports and dating, but even a busy adolescent has to have a day off.

"Want to go with me?" Dad was up to something and I knew you could expect anything on these spontaneous excursions. Spontaneous to me, but fully planned by my dad. He had called about a half-dozen people to join us at Dick and Mary Jo Looser's home to sing for Mary Jo's mom, Mrs. Estelle Poe. We sang and talked and had a hilarious good time topping it off with a good heartfelt prayer that left us all misty-eyed.

We did that in a couple of other homes that afternoon and added some more the next week. Thus began a new ministry to the sick and shut-ins because my dad got a big thrill out of doing things for people.

The Veteran

Little by little our World War II veterans are dying out. I don't know the latest statistics but there are not all that many left. Tom Brokaw calls them the greatest generation and I'm inclined to agree. They grew up during the Great Depression and fought a war and then came home and managed to build one of the greatest societies in human history. We owe a lot to these men and women who gave so much.

My Uncle Buddy Smelley was one of these veterans. He was a farm boy who grew up with his many brothers and sisters in the Mt. Olive area. Being the last of seven full siblings – the other six were girls – and having several more half-brothers and sisters he inherited quite a clan. Count'em all up and they number fourteen and when you throw in the steps the number swells to nineteen. And all nineteen had a tremendous respect for Joseph (Buddy) Smelley. I know I did. I don't know of a single person on this planet whom I admire more.

I never heard Uncle Buddy talk about the war. A lot of veterans don't. I learned about his service when I saw a picture of him in full uniform brandishing a bayonet and taking the charge stance. He served somewhere near the Aleutian Islands during the war, just a kid who was doing his duty. Uncle Sam called and Uncle Buddy served.

When Uncle Buddy came home from the war he used the money he got on his discharge to buy an army truck. He was going into the logging business. And he did haul logs in that old truck, but he expanded the use of that army vehicle for other purposes.

Such as dating Opal Harless. She was a girl who lived down the road and when Uncle Buddy got friendly with her he started driving her to the dances they both loved. He eventually drove that old truck across the state line into Mississippi to tie the knot when Aunt Opal was barely old enough to get married. I think about that every time I see an army truck.

Uncle Buddy and Aunt Opal got married shortly after I was born. That's why all my life I saw them together. They were inseparable. Together they raised a family of three boys – Wayne, Nicky and David - as well as provided a home for Aunt Opal's sister and three brothers –Sally and Bill and the twins, Olan and Noland. Because her mother was not always physically able to take care of the children Uncle Buddy and Aunt Opal stepped in and helped out. I was grown before I realized that her sister and brothers were not their children.

I was out at my Papa's farm one day hanging around my other uncles, Jerry and Thomas, when David came running by us being chased by Wayne and Nicky who were throwing dirt clod missles at the runaway. I said, "Boy, Uncle Buddy sure has his work cut out raising those boys."

Oh yes, they were a challenge! Like the time they decided to make their own booze. They sneaked around, bought the malt and sugar and whatever else they needed and then confiscated Aunt Opal's five gallon churn and started production up in the woods. These moonshiners were eventually caught, not by the local revenoors, as Snuffy Smith would say, but by their mother who finally had sniffed out their operation. She gave them a verbal licking that would qualify for the scolding award in the Guiness Book of World Records and then told Uncle Buddy who gave them another kind of licking that I'm sure qualifies for something.

Uncle Buddy was up to every challenge these boys - and life in general - hurled his way. He never gave up and he never gave in. He just worked hard and used the common sense the good Lord gave him and built quite a life for himself and those he loved.

Uncle Buddy made me realize how important ordinary people are to this country of ours. He never went to college. He never enjoyed a prestigious position. Every job he ever had involved dirt and sweat and a lot of muscle. But all this man did was serve his country in wartime and then work like crazy to provide for his family. And because of that self-sacrificing spirit I salute him. I salute all our veterans who have displayed that same spirit. In my book they are all

extraordinary.

Celebrating the Fourth

It's an old joke but I still laugh at it. A boy sat in his history class and was asked by his teacher who signed the Declaration of Independence. He shifted his feet and cleared his throat before blurting out, "It wasn't me, teacher. I didn't do it!"

The teacher was so upset that she called the boy's father and told him what the boy had said in answer to her question and the man replied, "If he says he didn't sign it then he didn't sign it. He's an honest boy."

Evidently he was also an ignorant boy.

When I was a kid I don't guess I gave much thought to the meaning of the Fourth of July or the signing of the Declaration of Independence. To me it was just a day of fun – swimming in the cool creek on a hot sunny day or playing a hot and sweaty ballgame before going to some relative's house to eat all the hamburgers and homemade ice cream that we could woof down.

Fourth of July! Time to celebrate. So on this special day we all hop into a car and follow my Uncle W. G. Snider down a little dirt road somewhere in Cedar Cove, Alabama, a little community a few miles northeast of Tuscaloosa and a place that Uncle W. G. always vowed and declared was heaven on earth. He grew up here.

We travel that dirt road that keeps narrowing until it turns into nothing more than a pig trail and becomes impassable. We get out and all of us guys walk through a little patch of woods to a wide place in the creek. We sit on the bank while the gals on the other side of the woods change into their swimsuits.

As soon as they finish we swap places until we are all decked out in our swimming attire ready for a great time of splashing around in the cold water and diving off a big rock (my specialty was the cannon ball) that overlooks the little pool in the creek.

After a few hours of such water games we go through the changing ritual again and then head back to civilization for our July fourth feast of every kind of food you can imagine.

As I said, this is what the Fourth meant to me as a kid. I was as ignorant of the true meaning of Independence Day as that boy and his father were of the signing of the Declaration. Since then I have learned a few things about why we celebrate this special day in the life of our nation. I learned that fifty-six men signed the famous document and pledged their lives, their fortunes and their sacred honor for the cause of freedom. Many of them made the ultimate sacrifice while others spent their entire fortune for the cause.

I think about that now. I also think about the many men and women who since then have pledged and given their lives so that we can enjoy life, liberty and the pursuit of happiness. That's why whenever I hear the National Anthem and see the flag going up the pole I stand at attention – whatever is going on around me and whatever other people are doing.

We still get together for fun, family and food. I still try to eat as many hamburgers as I can and I still go back for that second and third helping of the homemade ice cream. But now I am aware that this day means so much more. I know that I'm enjoying these fun times because of what some people so long ago and not so long ago did to make all these celebrations possible.

That's why I am a whole-hearted flag-waving unapologetic patriot. Always have been and always will be. Yes, I know that our America is not perfect. Neither am I. Neither are you. But we expect people to respect us and would be offended if they didn't. Yes, I know that we have many things to work on in this country to make it better and to live up to the ideals spelled out in the Declaration of Independence. But the flag stands for freedom and if we can't respect that and the people who made it so, then we can't respect anything.

I Used To Be My Own Grandpa

"Hello, I'm Billy Gray." I was introducing myself to someone somewhere sometime.

"Do you by chance know Wesley Gray?" That is a simple and understandable question but what the interrogator doesn't realize is that my answer is about to plunge him into a dark hole of confusion.

"I do know Wesley Gray. As a matter of fact Wesley is kin to me on my mother's side. He's her brother which makes him my uncle." I am being straight up honest.

I can see confusion beginning to creep in. "But I thought you said that your name is Gray which means your daddy is a Gray so how can Wesley Gray be your uncle on your mother's side?"

It is a sensible question for sure. I often wondered about that myself before I was old enough to figure out stuff. I respond, "You are right – my daddy is a Gray. His name is Leroy Gray."

The man standing before me is getting deeper into confusion. I am chuckling inside. I live for these moments when I can confuse people with my family history.

"But Leroy Gray is Wesley's brother and you say that Wesley is your uncle on your mother's side which would make Leroy your uncle, too, and yet you're telling me that Leroy is your daddy. So your daddy is your uncle?" By now he is scratching his head really hard.

I say, "Not really. Let me explain."

But before I can begin to unwind this family knot the man exclaims, "Oh, I get it! Your mother was a Gray who married a Gray." I guess it never dawns on him that while that will solve part of the puzzle it will make my mother marrying her brother. The old boy just seems quite pleased with himself that he has figured it out.

He has figured out nothing. I almost hate to tell him because I know it will drive the poor man to the brink of insanity. But this is too much fun to pass up. "No, my mother was a Smelley who married a Gray. But Wesley Gray is her brother and thus my uncle. And Leroy is my uncle and Leroy is my dad. And no, I have not been drinking."

"Man, you have one more confusing family," says the man with the puzzled face.

"You don't know the half of it. My mother has a brother-in-law who is also her uncle so that makes the man my uncle and great-uncle at the same time."

Now he thinks I'm lying. I see what's going through his mind. He's thinking – This boy has a real problem. He's lost touch with reality. I better get out of here as fast as I can. And as he turns and walks toward his car I yell, "Don't you want to hear about my cousin who is also my brother?"

Apparently he doesn't. And I confess I made that one up. But all the rest is true – just as true as it can be. And if this sounds confusing blame it on my granddaddy, Nicholas Smelley. He had three wives and children by each wife. My mom belonged to the middle set. And when Papa (as everybody in the family called him), being twice widowed, married the last time he chose a woman who had been married to a Gray and thus brought her Gray children into the family. And two of those sons were Wesley and Leroy, my mom's step-brothers and thus my step-uncles. And it just so happened that when my mom decided to get married she chose another Leroy Gray.

Is that all clear? Good. Now about this man who was both my mother's brother-in-law and uncle. Jimmy Brown was married to my mom's half-sister, Willie Bell. That made him my mom's brother-in-law. Uncle Jimmy was also brother to my mom's mother but no blood kin to Aunt Willie Bell who had a different mother. That made him my mom's uncle. Thus this man had the distinction of being both my uncle and great-uncle. Simple, huh?

Now let me tell you how I used to be my own grandpa...

Driver's Ed

Jumpity-jumpity-jerk-a-jerk. That's our old straight shift '53 Chevy that I'm trying to drive. I'm almost sixteen and like all kids my age I'm dying to get my driver's license. So I'm out on some deserted stretch of highway with my dad by my side trying to learn from this man how to handle this machine. I haven't yet managed to shift the gears with ease.

"Now with your foot on the clutch step lightly on the gas pedal," Dad says. Vroom vroom! I sound like I'm taking off at the Indy 500. "Not that much." I ease off a little. "Now as you step on the accelerator let out on the clutch." That's when the jumpity-jumpity-jerk-a-jerk comes in. I haven't figured out how to do the two things at once so we're bouncing all over the highway and suddenly the engine dies.

Sitting in the middle of the highway Dad leans over and says without any hint of panic, "Crank her up again." I do and we're off to the races. Well, we're off to somewhere. I finally learn to keep it going long enough to shift from low to second and then after a few more bumpy and sputtering attempts I manage to shift that baby from second to high. Pretty soon I'm in business. I'm driving. It's a rough ride all right but at least I can get that old vehicle from point A to point B.

The day arrives when I turn the magic number so I show up at the courthouse to get my license. But they send me home without the coveted prize. Something about what I said when the lady told me to look at the eye chart. I said, "What chart?" The one on the wall over there. "What wall?"

So I have to wait a few weeks until I can see the world well enough to be allowed out on the road. I don't understand that because I learned to drive without the specs so what's the big deal? But I have to admit that it is kind of nice to see the actual stoplight instead of just a blur in the sky. I didn't know what I had been missing. I can now tell if a light is red or green or yellow. Kinda nice to know when you're driving around town.

I actually show up for the driving part of the test in my Uncle's '54 Oldsmobile. I ditched the Chevy because the Olds is an automatic and I figure that if I can save the license examiner from a jumpity-jumpity-jerk-a-jerk ride it will be better for him. I'm just thoughtful that way, I guess. After all, he's an old man. I bet he's sixty if he's a day.

The only concern I have in this vehicle is the windshield wipers. My uncle believed in just making do instead of actually fixing things so when the knob that controls the wipers came off he just attached a box wrench to the stud. But I'm not worrying much about that because it's such a sunny day.

So here I am driving along the street with my license examiner calling out various vehicle maneuvering instructions. Everything is going fine until the unimaginable happens.

"Turn left at this next intersection." Nowhere in the manual does it say what to do when a car is coming up on the wrong side of the road where you're supposed to turn. I start sweating bullets but stop short of panic mode and for better or worse I swallow hard and wheel it in there and we keep moving. No comment from my official sidekick. Maybe he's in shock. So I guess I dodged that bullet.

Everything's going fine until the unimaginable happens. Again. It starts raining.

Rain? On a sunny day? Are you kidding me? Rain means wet windshield. Wet windshield means wiper blades. My mind focuses on the wrench. I'm afraid. I'm sweating. What if the wrench falls off? What if it stays on but he notices there is no knob? What if the wipers stop wiping? The "what ifs" are eating me up!

Should I break the silence and blurt out, "I know there is no knob! I know that I should have had it fixed! I know that you should probably fail me but I'm a good boy who's never stolen anything in his life except that time I took some unauthorized apples from Mrs. Rhodes' tree but my dad disciplined me and I have walked the straight and narrow ever since! And if you'll just pass me I promise that I'll spend the rest of my life hauling little old ladies back and forth to the doctor."

But I say nothing. I just keep driving, ignoring the wet stuff that is now pelting the windshield harder and harder. Mr. Examiner looks over at me and grunts, "Aren't you going to turn your wipers on?" I simply nod yes and reach over and twist the wrench while silently sending up the universal prayer, "Please!" The wipers come on, the wrench stays put and he says nothing. But he's writing like crazy and I know I'm doomed. He's failing me for an ill-equipped vehicle.

Finally, the test is over. Oh, well, it was a good run. Maybe next time.

I park it and we get out. Mr. Examiner hands me the paper and congratulates me on being a newly licensed driver. And because it's raining he never sees my tears of joy. He just thinks this wet stuff on my cheeks is the rain hitting my face.

The Dynamic Duo...Well, Sort of

"I better be ready. It's coming. If he keeps throwing the old ball that fast I'm gonna have to have a hand transplant." Those were my thoughts as Roland Brown readied himself to pitch another one of those hand scorchers. He was on the mound and I was behind the plate. Two guys – pro type pitcher and a catcher that didn't even qualify for amateur – re-enacting bull pen moments across the street on the vacant lot our neighborhood had reserved for various sports functions.

Roland went into his underhand windup and all of a sudden that ball came out of his hand whistling through the air ninety to nothing and...pop! Right into my very inadequate glove. Of course, it burned like crazy.

Roland said, "Did it sting?"

Of course it did. And I wanted to cry. But trying to appear as macho as possible I swallowed hard and said, "Nah, throw me another one." And for the next hour or so he popped that mitt so hard that my hand thought this was the beginning of WWIII. I know – it told me so – the rest of the night throbbing in a soaking solution.

Roland played in the heyday of fast-pitch softball here in good old Tuscaloosa. Maybe he couldn't hurl that softball as fast as Hall of Famers Paul Morrison or Ray Toler (who could?) but my hand certainly wasn't convinced. He was good, very good - one member of an arsenal of pitchers who flung that ball at upwards of a hundred miles an hour. Or so it seemed.

So why was I playing catch with this six-five guy who could wind up and chunk that old ball about as fast as lightning? Why was a kid not old enough (or good enough) to play with these pros trying to hang onto every ball this seasoned veteran threw at him?

It s simple. Roland Brown was my brother-in-law. And a little boy likes to do things with his grownup brother-in-law.

Here's the explanation of how I happened to be in this situation. Roland loved to eat.

Here's the explanation of why face feeding translated into baseball catching. My mom had cooked a big sumptuous meal and had invited my sister, Melna, and her new husband over. And like all newly-weds they were back at our house taking full advantage of a free and delicious meal.

One thing I had discovered about Roland Brown is that nobody was going to match him in a contest of putting it away. Years later I would witness this man with the cast iron stomach doing something I could never do and live to tell about it.

That happened the night before we were to fly out of Huntsville to Miami. We were eating out at Chili's and I was being oh so careful what I consumed, not wanting a queasy stomach on the flight. I hate to throw up on people forty thousand feet above ground. And when I looked over at Roland downing a big awesome blossom onion all by himself - that was just his appetizer - my stomach did somersaults just thinking about eating one of those spicy dishes. But my brother–in-law went home and slept like a baby and the next morning was in tip-top shape and ready to eat a big breakfast of eggs and sausage and ham and grits and...you get the idea. I mean he could put away anything you set before him and never suffer one smidgen of indigestion. My stomach hates people like that.

Back to the bull pen story. After such a sumptuous meal Roland looked at me and asked, "Want to chunk the old apple around a while?" Wowee! Of course! I agreed without consulting my hand in the matter. A mistake I was soon to find out. No doubt all that food he had been consuming had gone to his arm.

I had always wondered who my big sister would wind up marrying. I mean, there were always guys hanging around our house, much to her delight and Mom's consternation. I never did actually take bets on who would be my future brother-in-law but, as I said, I wondered. And it turned out to be Roland Brown. And in that moment behind the plate I wondered if my sister had made the right choice. Should she have married a guy who throws like a girl? Nah, my hand may have been better off but my family wouldn't. I wouldn't take anything for having Roland Brown as my brother-in-law.

With such a voracious appetite Roland certainly married the right woman. My sister is one of the best cooks anywhere. Every time I have gone to her house for a meal my mouth starts salivating two hours before I get there. She knows how to put it on the table all right. Maybe that was the secret to their fifty-four years of marriage, a marriage that lasted until Roland passed away a couple of years ago.

I miss those days on the diamond trying to catch a softball missle. I miss going out to eat and watching my brother-in-law consume the spiciest dishes without a hint of any digestive discomfort. I really miss him picking up the check every time telling me, "Preachers don't make any money so I've got this. You just worry about preaching to those sinners." I miss him bragging to everybody at the reception how good I did singing the Lord's Prayer at his daughter's wedding when I know I sounded like a reject from the American Idol audition.

Roland Brown. Fun guy to be with. Good man. Great brother-in-law.

A New House but an Old Home

When I was growing up we rented our house...until we built one of our own. Actually, we lived in six places where we paid money to the landlord before Dad decided one day, "Whoa! Enough of this! Let's build our own house and build up our own equity."

I was about sixteen when the declaration was made and I remember how excited I was especially when I learned that this house would have a full basement. I was thinking "man cave" before I had ever heard that term and before I was even a man. I could just see me and my buddies hanging out in a place away from the rest of the family doing man stuff.

However, my excitement cooled somewhat when I learned that building our own house meant that I would have to do some of the work. I wasn't exactly allergic to work - I just tried to get out of it every chance I could. It's something that's in the male teen genes. But work I did! As Dad constantly said, "Every nail that we drive saves us paying someone else for that labor." I had to remind myself of that every time I dug a ditch or hammered the wrong nail.

Every Saturday whether Dad was there or not (sometimes he had to work a shift at the Paper Mill) I joined Johnny Smelley, our builder, and his brother-in-law, Buddy Faulkner, and Buddy's dad to work on the house. I thought maybe Johnny, being my first cousin, would cut me some slack. I was wrong. Johnny believed in working hard. That wasn't the problem. He also believed that everybody on the job should work hard. That was the problem. At least it was for this sixteen year old kid who kept thinking of the ball games he was missing or the relaxing times sitting on the front porch swing watching the ebb and flow of neighborhood life.

"Billy, what are you doing standing around down there? "Pop goes my day dream bubble! Johnny was calling to me from the rooftop. I wanted to answer – "I'm nursing my blistered hands" or "I'm trying to think of a way I can escape" or "I worked up a big sweat handing those boards up to ya'll and I'm thinking of quitting." But I didn't say any of those things. I just climbed up on the roof with all the other workers and started nailing away. Half the time I didn't know what I was doing so if you pass by our old home place today and see a part of the roof sagging that was the part I was working on.

But cousin Johnny was very good. If he noticed that I was having trouble with something he'd stop what he was doing and come over and show me how. And then he would walk away just like he fully expected me to get busy doing what he had just showed me to do. Just like I was some kind of adult. Just like I was one of his workers. Just like I was getting paid for this (which I wasn't but as Dad said every nail driven saves us money).

All in all it was a great experience and many years later when I spoke at Johnny's funeral I told the family how glad I was that I had that opportunity to work under him. He knew his business and he knew how to deal with a sometimes slacker like me.

We moved into our new house and the next year I graduated from TCHS. But I still hung around for a few more years enjoying this house that I helped put together. I stuck around until something better than a new house came along. I'm talking about my new wife, Margaret Ann.

My dad enjoyed this house that he put so much into, but fourteen years later on a Christmas Eve he drove away for the last time before losing his life in an auto accident. My mom continued to live there until she surprised us all by moving to Huntsville when she was eighty-three (as she explained to me, "I just want to see the grandkids every day). I thought she would boo-hoo all over the place as we drove her away that last time. But it was her son who did all the crying. Mom never looked back.

I look back all the time. And every once in awhile I drive by the old house and a little tear sometimes slides down my face as I thank God, not for the house, but for the home we had there.

Around the Supper Table

My dad knew that Mom was sweet on another man. He could see it in her eyes as he watched her watch him. Well, Mom's infatuation was no secret at our house but it all came to a head one evening at the supper table. Mom was going on and on about this man named Cheyenne Bodie who was a character played by Clint Walker on the popular television series, Cheyenne.

Dad interrupted her streak of praise for the great one saying, "I don't think Cheyenne Bodie is so great." And with that he began to mimic the Cherokee man's talk and then got up and started strutting around the room in his best Cheyenne gait. Talk about an academy award performance! There was no doubt about that.

But Mom wasn't about to sit still while Dad was making fun of her hero. She blurted out, "You better wish that you were half the man Cheyenne Bodie is." We were shocked at what came out of Mom's mouth but in a nanosecond we were all losing it rolling all over the floor and laughing ourselves silly. Dad and Mom and children sharing a time of levity at Dad's star performance and the idea of our parents poking fun at each other over a man who didn't exist. And it all happened at the supper table – the eating hour – the entertainment hour – the discussion hour.

Yes, discussion. We always ate together as a family and as we were closing in on the clean plate award we started talking about whatever needed talking about. Sometimes it was on the silly side - like Cheyenne's effect on the female half of our parents - but sometimes the discussion was more serious. "Mama, make Billy stop aggravating me." That was my kid sister, Marcille, complaining - as if I would ever do such a thing as try to make her life miserable. Okay, there was that time...

But then Mom and Dad would take this as a teachable moment. "Son, you better get it together if you know what's good for you." And I always did know what was good for me – a switch or belt if I didn't improve my social skills with my sisters.

And this learning all took place at the supper table.

What was really interesting was when the discussion concerned my other sister, Melna, who arrived at teenage status four years before I did. And you know what being a teenage girl means – boys. That meant that the supper table discussion sometimes got very interesting. My sister was a boy magnet and consequently we had guys hanging around our house all the time. It made for some pretty interesting moments. Like the time two boyfriends showed up for a date with her at the same time.

How did that happen and what do you do when that happens? My mom knew the answer to that last part - you send them home – and then she went to work on that first part escorting sis into the other room and closing the door behind them. This was going to be a discussion not meant for the table. It was censored for the younger set. So I had to put my ear up against the door and really strain to hear it all.

Sometimes table time was correction time. The only thing is that when you correct somebody it can backfire on you. Mom looks over at Marcille and tells her that she needs to curb her sweets to which kid sister responds by making the sound of a car swerving to avoid hitting a curb. I think that's just her way of getting Mom off her back. And to this day I don't know why that admonition because my sister has never had a weight problem and was probably the healthiest of all of us.

Now picture this – Mom is lecturing her daughter about sweets and Marcille says, "I challenge anybody in this family to show that you've eaten less of the sweet stuff than I have." So here we are taking inventory of our sugar intake for the last two weeks. That's right – we're mentioning dishes and names and places and the next thing you know Mom is defending herself by saying, "The last time I had a regular size piece of pie was at Dorothy Camp's." And ever since then none of us can bite into a piece of pie without saying it – "The last time I had a regular size piece of pie..." and then in unison we fill in the rest.

It's a reminder of something that we cherish – sharing life around the supper table. And remembering Dorothy Camp's regular size piece of pie.

A Backseat View of Our Vacation Trip

I hate we have to but if you have to you just have to. It's a long trip of five hundred miles and we somehow have to occupy our time or else go crazy. Okay, so we're not thinking too much of our parents' sanity as we belt out one ridiculous song after another cruising down the highway in our 1953 Chevrolet from Northport, Alabama to Gainesville, Florida. It's going to be five hundred miles of fun, fun and more fun!

"We're here because we're here because we're here because we're here – same song second verse, gotta get better 'cause it can't get worse. We're here because we're here because we're here because we're here – same song third verse, gotta get better 'cause it can't get worse." And so it goes as we push that number of verses up into the hundreds before finally hearing a passionate plea coming from the front seat for us to do something else for awhile. Maybe count cars or something.

Are we there yet?

Okay, let's play a counting game. Not cars, but cows. And let's make it boys against girls. That sounds logical. After all we're still little kids and haven't yet discovered the fun of teaming up with the opposite sex. And besides, they're our sisters. Who wants to team up with your sister? Yuck!

That means that cousin Joe and I face off against sister Melna and cousin Sonja. Marcille, my little sister, is sitting in the front seat doing all she can to bug the daylights out of my mom and dad. Our cousins had come up on their vacation and had been left behind for a couple more weeks and now we're returning them home while enjoying our vacation. I have to hand it to my dad and Uncle James – they know how to have a cheap vacation – load up the whole family and head toward your relatives. But does Dad have to pack four of us in the back seat like we're a can of sardines? I have this recurring pain in my side where Joe's elbow is puncturing my ribs.

Are we there yet?

On with the game! "There's one...two...three...four...five... six. Six cows. How many have you girls got so far? None! Aww, that's too bad." We guys are very compassionate. Always. We love are sisters but I'll be doggone if we're going to let them beat us at anything. "Hey, Joe, look at all those cows all over that hillside. Let's get busy." And just like that we've added two dozen more cows to our herd. "How are you gals coming? Oh, just a half-dozen. So sad."

We're fools – Joe and me. We're rubbing it in just as if we're not aware that our cow fortune can change at any moment. And it does change in the blinking of an eye. Our side comes to a cemetery and we have to bury all our cows while at the same time the girls have hit the big time as we come upon the biggest herd of cattle I've ever seen. After awhile we start getting beat really bad (and there are few things in life worse than losing to your sister). I'm ready to quit. "Let's play something else", I moan.

Are we there yet?

How about let's sing "Ninety-nine bottles of beer on the wall"? And despite all the groans coming from the front seat everybody in the back seat is okay with it. I mean, this is the all-time favorite trip song ever. So we start. We sing it for the next two hundred miles. We sing it all the way down to that one bottle on the wall. But we don't just sing that last verse about the lone bottle – we drunk sing it. Meaning we act tipsy moving from side to side (which isn't easy packing four kids in a seat) while slowing it down and slurring

our words. Taaake one dowwwn…hic…pash it roun…hic…nooo
bottles of beer…hic… ooonnn the waaall…hic".

Are we there yet?

And from the front seat I hear some adult person say, "I wish
to goodness we were."

Renaissance Man

Renaissance man. That was Michelangelo. Sculptor, Painter,
Engineer, Scientist, Poet. This gifted man could do it all. Renaissance
man II. That would be my cousin, Douglas Holloway. Chess Master,
Rocket Scientist, Music Critic, Athlete, Sports Promoter. He could
do it all.

Chess Master. I had always been a checkers guy content
to mindlessly move the pieces across the board looking for my
opponent to crown me. Then Doug introduced me to the pleasures
of the game of chess. I didn't know a rook from a knight from a
bishop until Doug sat me down one day and described every piece
and the moves they could make. Once I had grasped the basics of
chess we played a game and so as not to discourage me the chess
master allowed me to win. I would make a dumb move and he'd
clear his throat and tell me to watch the other pieces on the board
and think about what they could do as a result.

Move…move…move. Checkmate! I was elated! I had won! I
had beaten the teacher! Okay, so he let me win in order to explain
the game and keep me interested. It was fun. But forever thereafter
it was a challenge to just stay in the game with Doug. I hardly ever
beat the master once he didn't have to let me win.

Rocket Scientist. Doug and Sonny Wright designed rockets
(from bottles and tin cans to more sophisticated looking inventions)
and experimented with ingredients for fuel to propel them. We
neighborhood boys sat in the kitchen watching Doug mix a little
sulfur, some saltpeter and sugar and who knows what else to make
a powerful fuel that would blow a rocket all the way over Mr. Plott's

house into the Sanders' yard. At least, that's what we were hoping to do so that when we went to fetch it we could catch a glimpse of the gorgeous Merline.

You never know what motivates a mad scientist. More often than not, our rocket went off in the other direction landing in the trees and on the rooftops and hedge bushes in Gus Beasley's yard.

The best rocket of all was one we never got to launch. Lloyd Junkin's mother conviscated it fearing that we were about to blow ourselves up if we tried to send that monster into space. She was right and it is probably due to her wisdom that we have all our limbs today.

Music Critic. Doug introduced me to classical music. I went from Grand Ole Opry to Metroplitan Opera in a matter of seconds sitting in Doug's room listening to records he had checked out of the library. He would put on Mario Lanza's rendition of "The Drinking Song" and turn to me and say, "Now listen to this last note. Mario is going to hit a note somewhere in the stratosphere." And I would adjust my ears to high volume and listen. And wait. And Mario would hit it.

Now I know why they call it music appreciation. I appreciated it. And enjoyed it so much that this teetotaler went home singing a drinking song.

Athlete. One of Doug's teachers told me, "The thing about Douglas is that he will make an A on his test and then go out and play football with the guys. He's a very well-rounded young man." I would go over to Doug's house and listen to him explain some complicated math problem and then go outside and watch him throw the discus or kick a football over the shed in his backyard. And I'd go to the game and watch him play tackle for TCHS and kick extra points for the team.

Sports Promoter: It wasn't enough for Doug to enjoy sports, he wanted the rest of us to participate, too. Which is why he bought some boxing gloves and enlisted every boy in the neighborhood to compete in a boxing tournament. And why he made a set of weights out of concrete and got all of us guys involved in a weight-lifting competition. He even worked out a formula so that we little guys could compete with the heavyweights.

As I said, he could do it all. So if you see Doug, ask him for the square root of 7921 and then hand him a football and go out for a pass. The Renaissance man will yell, "eighty-nine" and then hit you in the deep corner of the end zone. He can do it all.

X

Take This Job and Love It

The Coolest Job in the World

I KNOW YOU THINK you've eaten good ice cream but you don't know the meaning of good until you have had a scoop of Pure Process ice cream from right here in Tuscaloosa County.

Pure Process Ice Makers was the official name of the enterprise and I worked for them from the time I was thirteen all the way through high school. So did a lot of other Northport boys. Terry Beck and Grafton Pritchett and the Barger boys – Bobby, Joe and Marvin - come to mind. And I think Ken Kennedy worked there because I can remember Ken standing in the hall at TCHS commenting as I passed by – "There goes one of those Poor Progress boys." That was our favorite name for the establishment and we were always kidding each other about it although it was a pretty neat place for a boy to work.

I have some fond and some not so fond memories of working in that place. Here's one that was fond - getting to eat all the ice cream you wanted. Is that heaven on earth or what! Okay, if you ate too much Mr. Foster Norton, the owner, could give you the old evil eye. I don't ever remember his convicting eye looking my way because I was much too busy working to spend a lot of time consuming the delicious product. You do believe that, don't you?

Actually, for some reason Mr. Norton liked me. He had enough reasons not to. Such as the time I dropped one of those five gallon cans of ice cream and we all watched it bounce around the room with customers scattering trying to get out of the line of fire. And such as the time I couldn't find the store that had ordered twenty-five bags of ice and returned with melting ice under that tarp in the truck bed.

But he kept me on. I like to think it was because I was such a great worker but maybe it was because my uncle was the night manager there.

Well, for some reason Mr. Norton and I got along. When I was in college I worked there whenever they needed me and the boss would always inquire about how I was doing in my studies and encourage me to keep it up.

Like I say, I have fond memories.

But some were not so fond. I almost lost my hand in the ice crusher.

When we weren't dipping ice cream for the customers we were working out in the ice house manhandling three hundred pound blocks of ice. I guess that's the reason I have such rippling muscles today and am mistaken for Arnold Swartzwhoever. I guess that's why I won the local strong man contest three years in a row. Okay, I'm exaggerating. It was no years in a row. Or out of the row. And it wasn't old Arnold that was my mistaken identity. It was Barney Fife.

Back to the ice house incident. Here's what happened. We had to cut that massive ice block into several sections before throwing it a chunk at a time into the ice crusher. And sometimes if the chunk was too large the machine would stall.

When that happened I had seen other more experienced guys do something that I thought was dangerous. Just beat the ice with the tongs. While the machine was still on. Our ice house boss, Mr. Eual Free whom we all called Eskimo, had warned us not to do such a crazy thing.

But when you're a teenager sometimes the machine can be running while your mind is in neutral. Which explains the dumb thing I did that day. I beat the ice with the tongs without shutting off the machine. Mind in neutral, hand in machine.

I felt a jolt, but didn't realize the cutter in the machine had sliced across my left hand – after all, it was below freezing in the ice house - until I went outside and noticed my thawing hand starting to bleed. I went running into the office and the manager bound up my hand and carried me to the first aid area in the back of the meat-packing part of the plant.

You will be glad to know that I survived and am somewhere in the United States still consuming good ice cream to this very day.

Then I have some memories that are a mix of fond and not so fond. I was up front dipping that ice cream like nobody's business. It was a busy day and people were lined up all the way outside. We were going through can after can of those twenty featured flavors for which Pure Process was famous – vanilla fudge, black walnut, cherry garden, lemon custard, orange pineapple, cherry whitehouse, butter pecan, to name a few - when I noticed the gorgeous Annie Carol Warren walk through the door and stand just a few feet from me.

Now that was the fond part. But the closer she got the more nervous I became and when it was time for me to take her order I blurted out, "And what flavor cane...uh...I mean cone...do you please...I mean, want?" Plus suddenly my hand was all thumbs and I dropped my scoop somewhere around the vanilla fudge.

From fond to not so fond in a split second. But I must say on my behalf that I managed to retrieve my scoop and carry on just as if there was not this most gorgeous girl in the world standing in front of me. I had rebounded. We were trained for moments like this. Just ask any old Pure Process alumni. They're everywhere.

As I said, I bounced back from failure and today I can dip a scoop of ice cream even with several beauties all around me. Just ask my gorgeous granddaughters.

I Became a Horse Whisperer and Didn't Even Have Laryngitis

Once upon a time I didn't even know what a horse whisperer was and then I became one. The first time I ever heard the term I thought someone was talking about a horse with laryngitis. But then I became enlightened on the matter and started my career of breaking in horses. That career lasted a total of two hours.

Okay, let's turn back the clock and see how this happens.

Alfred Mitchell stops by our house one day and asks me if I would be interested in breaking in a few Shetland ponies he has recently acquired. What sixteen year old boy wouldn't love to ride horses? "Man oh man! Wow! Whoopee! When do I start?"

I'm all in.

Big mistake. I know next to nothing about Shetland ponies except that they're short and kind of cute. They say that ignorance is bliss and sometimes it is and sometimes it isn't. My ignorance about the Shetland ponies' ill-tempered nature is about to provide me with something considerably short of bliss.

I arrive at the pasture and look over at this other guy about my age strutting along on his pony just as calmly as you please. I think – this is going to be fun. Alfred brings my pony over to me and says, "Mount up." Which I do. And with a few helpful tips about how to handle such an animal I am on my way to a full cowboy experience.

In my innocent enthusiasm I yell, "Hi yo, Silver, away!" with visions of galloping off to rescue some damsel in distress. But old Silver has gone to a different school. He has other ideas. He's made up his mind that he is not going anywhere – distressed damsel or not.

I know the first order of business is to get this animal going. So I swat him with the reins and kick him in the sides and yell out, "Giddy up!" Nothing. It's foreign language to this stubborn creature and I'm thinking – where is Mr. Ed when you need him?

I dismount and walk around to the front of the horse and stare him right in the eyes. I saw Gene Autry's sidekick, Frog Millhouse, do that one time and it seemed to work. I then give that animal a little pep talk and get back on ready to set out on happy trails as Dale and Roy would say. Still nothing.

Now you know what happens when momma puts a whole dish of fried chicken on the table and you start drooling as you begin to gnaw on one of those chicken legs? That's what my leg must look like to this Shetland pony because when I swat him to giddy up he swings his head around and starts gnawing on my leg. I pull the reins tight to the other side and all he does is switch sides helping himself to leg of Billy. Without the garlic and herbs.

So here's this stubborn and confounded animal just standing there in idle but doing a lot of chewing. And Alfred looks over and sees what's going on and it makes him so mad that he tells me to get down. And I do. Then the fun really begins as six foot seven Alfred (and that's on one of his short days) mounts up determined to show that critter who is boss. He's straddle that pony with his legs touching the ground and what I see next is a tale for two cities and part of a country.

All of a sudden that pony bolts down the hillside just like he's out of the gate at the Kentucky Derby. I can almost hear the crowd going wild as both pony and rider beat it down that hill ninety to nothing with Alfred's legs dragging the ground as he is trying to hang on for dear life when all of a sudden that ornery pony comes to a dead stop and Alfred goes flying through the air...without a trapeze.

And I go home. I don't want to see a man kill a pony.

And the reason for the horse whispering is because I didn't want to tell this to anybody out loud.

Tractors R Us

It's my first day on the job and I'm a little bit nervous. After all, I know nothing about tractors. To tell the truth, I know next to nothing about anything. But here I am ready to start my new job at a tractor place. I forget the name of the outfit but I do remember that I am here because my dad had a friend who had a friend who owned this place.

No doubt when they were sitting around one day discussing who was going to be the next Governor and other vital issues my dad worked in this question, "Do you have any job that my kid could do?"

Now a smart man would have asked, "What can your kid do?" But apparently that subject was never broached because here I am completely clueless about anything except sports and eating and now I've got this job working with tractors. And that's good because I'm in college and somehow I have to pay to become an educated human being. And that's bad because I flunked tractor when I was in high school.

The man in charge leads me back to this shop that's cluttered with all kinds of machines and parts – crankshafts, generators, pistons, etc. He walks me over to a table on which sits a carburetor. I know that's what it is because he says, "Do you know anything about carburetors?" I don't and I tell him so. I read disappointment all over his face. So we get moving around the room and at each table I have to admit that I have no experience or knowledge of whatever it is that he is showing me.

Not knowing what to do the man in charge says, "Let's step out back." Surely he's not going to work me over just because I'm dumb. That's what I'm thinking as he opens this big door and we step into the great outdoors. And there before my eyes is a huge yellow Caterpillar road machine.

"Now I want you to get this baby ready to paint" and with that he hands me a wire brush and some sandpaper. "I want you to sand it and wash it and then we'll get somebody in here who knows what he is doing to paint it." I know right off who won't be doing the paint job.

This project takes several days and when my friends ask me what I'm doing over there at that tractor place I proudly say, "Right now I'm working on this road machine." Of course, every day I leave work dirty as a filthy pig and before going home and washing up I just happen to drop by to see my friends. That way they can see how hard I've been working and conclude that I got that way doing mechanic work – a conclusion I kind of help along by dropping terms that I have picked up listening to the other fellows at the tractor place.

One day I go in and the man in charge says, "I think you've done all that you can do on that Caterpillar. Come with me." What now? Is it over? He asks me if I'm any good at math and when I tell him that I am (I can say all my multiplication tables with my eyes closed and one hand tied behind my back) he leads me to an office and hands me several sheets and instructs me to add these columns. I do so – without a calculator or so much as an adding machine. I spend the next several days working in this little office and when I happen up on my friends who notice that I have left work clean as a whistle I explain, "I've been promoted to the front office."

And that's where I work for the remainder of my tenure there – which is two weeks. The man in charge walks in and says, "I'm sorry, we're going to have to let you go." Translation – "We can't find anything else that a know-nothing nincompoop can do and we just hired you because your dad's friend of a friend said that you needed a little money for college so this is our contribution."

And that's okay with me. Especially when I look at my check. They have been very generous. And I am forever grateful to this man who let me work at his tractor place while knowing nothing about tractors. Except that they get dirty and need washing every now and then.

My Record-breaking Coaching Career

I hold a record that not even Nick Saban can approach. I lost every game I ever coached. My coaching career started way back in the second grade. That's when the seed was planted for my launching a coaching career that would last forever. At least, that's how long that season seemed to the players…and their parents… and to me.

Here's the story. It all goes back to when I was a seven year old attending our school's Halloween Carnival. I was having fun bobbing for apples and running through the haunted house and collecting a load of candy when I decided to visit the fortune teller. So I walked behind a spooky curtain into a dark room and was introduced to this gypsy looking woman who started gazing into a crystal ball.

She whispered, "You are going to be a football coach." How did she know that was my greatest ambition? That and being a truck driver. I assumed the crystal ball let her in on my little secret.

I never realized that prediction would come true but ten years later there I was courtside as my team of church boys took to the hardwood for the first time. Okay, so it wasn't football. Cut the lady a little slack, will you! Maybe the batteries on her crystal ball were running low. That sometimes happens. But the important thing is that I was fulfilling a life-long dream – I was coaching.

I had come a long way. Ten miles to be exact. That's how far it was from my house to the Calvary Baptist Church gymnasium. My boys were pumped. I was pumped. We had enthusiasm! We had fight! We had everything but talent.

First game. I send them out to the middle of the court for the tip-off. And away we go.

Wait! What is this? Why is Tim just standing around out there? He looks like he thinks he's a spectator. "Hey ref, time out!"

The boys huddle around me. "Okay, Tim, you have to move around out there. You can't just stand in one place all the time. You came to play…so let's play." Tim nods. He's ready.

Off they go. What I see next can only be described as…as…as unbelievable. Tim is moving around, all right, but in no relation to the game. He's just dancing away in center court. No matter that the action is under the goal. He keeps dancing in the half-court circle as if he thinks he's at the prom.

"Hey ref, time out!"

I have to talk with Tim. "Tim…boy…son, you see this puzzled look on my face? That's because I'm puzzled – what are you doing out there?"

"Well, you told me to move around." Yes, I did. I really did. The kid is right. So I explain to this wannabe basketball player that I mean for him to move toward the guy who has the ball. Guard him. Keep him from scoring. Get the rebound when it comes off the goal. That's what I mean when I say move around. Tim nods. He understands. He's ready.

Okay, we're in. Somehow Tim gets the ball. I told him to move so he's moving. With the ball! Without dribbling! He's just running down the court with the ball tucked under his arm like he's playing football! The ref blows the whistle. "Traveling."

"Hey ref, time out!"

I look over at Tim, this time with a look of desperation added to my puzzled countenance. Huddle time again. "Yes, Tim, I saw you moving. You even got the ball. Great job. But Tim, you have to dribble the ball as you advance it or they'll call you for traveling. Do you understand?" He does. We're okay. He's ready.

And so it went. For the whole season.

By season's end Tim had learned a whole lot - about what not to do. So had I. Again, about what not to do. We lost every game but one – the one I missed due to sickness. At the end of the season I resigned for the same reason. Sickness. Everybody was sick of my coaching.

The Conclusion of the Whole Matter

You Don't Have to be Good at Stuff to Enjoy Life

LITTLE BOYS GET STARS in their eyes and visualize being great at something. I know I did. But over time I came to realize that I'm just your ordinary guy. And that's okay with me. I've always had fun anyway.

Sometimes a bunch of us boys would put a dead limb between two trees and see how high we could jump. Some of the fellows would go soaring over the high bar while some would struggle to get over the low one. Guess which group I was in? But I think I had as much fun as the high jumpers. It's just that I kept my laughing closer to the ground. Nothing wrong with that!

Choose any sport you like and honesty will compel me to confess that I was always in the middle of the pack. Not too good but not too bad either.

Take baseball for instance. I don't think I'd be stretching the truth by telling you that I could do some things well but when it came to overall ability on the diamond I never stood out from the other fellows. For one thing, I always had trouble judging a ball coming toward me. Some guy at the plate would hit that old cowhide to the outfield and I'd run up on it only to watch it sail over my head and plop down about fifteen feet behind me.

165

"My mistake", I'd yell. "I'll get it next time!" But when next time came I'd backpedal only to watch the ball fall to the ground about fifteen feet in front of me.

"Can't that stupid ball make up its stupid mind where it's going to land on this stupid field?" I know that's a lot of stupid but you get how I felt.

However, as I said, I wasn't a total washout. I was good at some things. I could run fast. Maybe not as fast as our TCHS state champ, the fleet-footed Johnny Kirkley (who could?). Or the track stars in my class - such as Wade Booth, Harry Nichols, Richard Hulsey and Jerry Parker. But I could put it into high gear when I had a mind to. I prided myself on being able to beat out an infield grounder. That was good because I rarely hit one to the outfield. How boring would that be! Anyone can beat out a grounder to the outfield. I hate to brag but I never hit it over any infielder's head.

Fast forward twenty-five years. I'm at the plate. Our church is playing another church on a Sunday night. It's August and our two churches, Taylorville Baptist and Little Sandy Baptist, are having joint services out at the Taylorville ball field. I stand on the mound and deliver a message (get it – deliver...) and the next Sunday night Marvin Palmer does the same. Then we eat. And then we play.

Tonight's game is softball. They let me go first. Is it because they know what a powerful hitter I am or is it because they just want to get the worst out of the way? I'm opting for the powerful hitter explanation.

The first pitch comes (I've always been a sucker for swinging at the first pitch - probably for some deep psychological reason that nobody can understand). This time I connect and the ball goes bouncing out to the shortstop. He catches it on the first hop but that doesn't bother me.

Remember my pride? I've got this. I'll just beat the ball to first! But suddenly I make a discovery. With two to follow. Discovery number one – I lack starting power. For some reason my head knows I ought to be running but my feet are yet to get the message.

However, my feet finally pick up on the head vibes and I'm off and running and that is when I make my second discovery – I lack stopping power. I fly past first base - the ball has already arrived and the guys are chunking it around the infield waiting on the next batter – but I can't stop until I get way out in right field. That plop, thud sound is this famous runner making his third discovery – I have an abundance of stumbling power. I hit the turf and plow up the outfield better than a ditch witch.

Yes, I'm just your average Joe. And that's okay because I have made another discovery. You don't have to be good at stuff in order to have the time of your life.

So I wasn't at the top of my class academically. But I've had fun telling people that I'm like the guy whose teacher asked him to conjugate a verb and he thought she was talking dirty because he didn't know what conjugate meant.

So I sat on the bench all football season and loaned my uniform out piece by piece. But I've had fun joking about how I was a no count player whose uniform made All-American.

So I've never made a lot of money nor do I live in the ritzy part of town. But I've had fun joking and paling around with the salt of the earth kind of friends and neighbors who have made my life rich.

So I've never been invited to preach at any of the big pastor's conferences. But I've had fun preaching to my little flock of people who love me and tell people that they have the best pastor in town.

Some wise man once said, "If at first you don't succeed, try, try again." That's a great quote. But here's how I'd put it - "If at first you don't succeed, just grin, make a joke of it and move on." You'll have everybody in your corner in no time.

Printed in the United States
By Bookmasters